Fatbiking across Mongolia

A 2000 kilometre bikepacking adventure

Thank you to all of the Mongolian nomads who supported Phil and me during our adventure. The respect you have for your country was humbling and your selflessness and desire to help others were inspirational and invaluable to us.

First published in the UK by Tom Bruce

www.tombrucecycling.com

Contents

Introduction 3

The journey to kilometre zero 5

Day 1: Into to the land of the nomads 9

Day 2: The swamp 18

Day 3: Mountain passes and Üüreg Nuur 26

Day 4: To Ulaangom 32

Day 5: The Gobi Desert 38

Day 6: Across more steppe 45

Day 7: A plague of locusts and a storm 53

Day 8: Into the heartland 58

Day 9: Nomad hospitality 66

Day 10: Goulash and buuz 76

Day 11: The best camp 83

Day 12: It was going so well... 89

Day 13: Motorbike bearing bodge 95

Day 14: Khövsgöl Nuur 101

Day 15: Camping on Khövsgöl Nuur 105

Day 16: Off the beaten track 110

Day 17: Trails, trails, trails 117

Day 18: Wet, wet, wet 124

Day 19: The longest day 127

Day 20: Bulgan 132

Day 21: Erdenet 137

Day 22: Off-road again 142

Day 23: Trailblazing 146

Day 24: Total washout 153

The trans-Mongolian railway and Ulan-Uud 155

Looking back on the trip, one year on 160

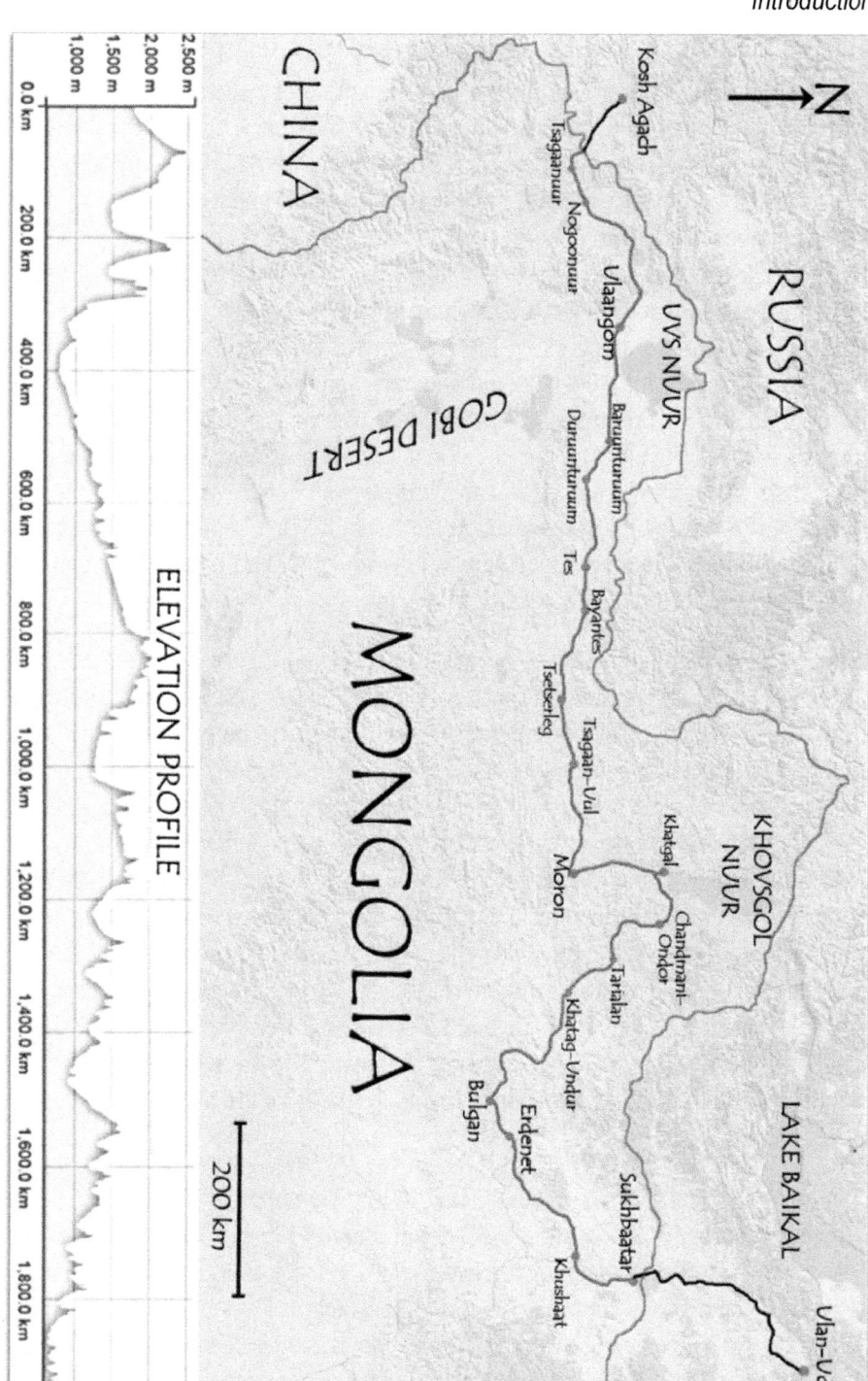

Kosh Agach to Ulan-Ude

ELEVATION PROFILE

3

Introduction

Five years ago I cycled around the world. It was the greatest adventure of my life and provided countless experiences, which I now look back on with a mixture of fondness and pride. However, there was something missing from my trip. The country that I had most wanted to visit was Mongolia. I spent hours poring over satellite images and reading about various routes across the country. My plan had been to cycle north across Kazakhstan, then cycle across the small part of Russia that separates Mongolia from Kazakhstan. Although their borders come within about 40 kilometres of each other, the only way to enter Mongolia from the west was via Russia. Unfortunately, bureaucratic embassy officials and overly complicated application processes meant that I was unable to get a Russian visa from an embassy outside of the UK. Since I was in Uzbekistan at the time of application, visiting a UK embassy was clearly not an option. As a result, I ended up having to change my route and cycled across China rather than Mongolia. Although this was a fantastic adventure in its own right, I had always regretted not being able to travel through Mongolia...

Mongolia sounded like paradise. A vast unspoilt nation full of nomads and their animals with endless grasslands inhabited by herds of wild horses. I imagined clear blue rivers full of fish, surrounded by snow-capped mountains and a land without boundaries and complete freedom for its inhabitants. I wanted to visit Mongolia more than anywhere else in the world. Fortunately (although not entirely coincidentally) my new career as a teacher includes long summer holidays, which I intended to use that year to cycle across the country. My cousin Phil was also free during the summer and we had both bought fatbikes, which are mountain bikes with very wide tyres. They would be perfect for cycle touring on the remote tracks in Mongolia. We had purchased them especially for this trip but I had spent the past two winters cycling mine in the Peak District. I had also had a brilliant adventure during my previous summer holiday, riding it across the Balearic islands. I was very much looking forward to trying it out for the purpose for which it had been built.

I had unfinished business in Mongolia and I was very happy to be travelling there with Phil, who had been a perfect travelling companion when we cycled across China. We had cycled together for two months on a route just a few hundred kilometres south of the one that we would be riding in Mongolia. After a crazily busy year, the summer holidays crept up on me and a few late evenings of last-minute planning crammed in during the last week of term helped prepare for

4

departure. As ever the plan was not made in great detail, although we had decided upon a rough route and I had created a GPS file to follow, which would help with navigation. We were ready for another adventure.

The journey to kilometre zero

Mongolia is not a particularly common travel destination from England, nor in fact from anywhere else. There is only one international airport in the capital city, Ulanbaatar, connected to England via Russia, China or Kyrgyzstan with long waits in airports. We wanted to cycle across the country on an *A to B* route, rather than a round loop so ideally needed to fly into one airport and out from another. Cycling from one place to another is much more satisfying than a round loop because it feels like you are going somewhere. Motivation is higher and working out daily distance targets as well as an overall schedule is much easier. The only way for us to achieve this was to fly in and out of Mongolia's more developed neighbour, Russia. Russia's flight infrastructure is extensive, with most cities having a well-connected airport, served by budget airlines (just don't look up their safety record). We planned to fly into the city of Barnaul, close to the Altai Mountain Range, cross the border into the far west of Mongolia, cycle across the country to the north-east and cross back into Russia, and then fly home from the city of Ulan-Ude.

This wasn't quite as easy as it sounds. To enter Russia twice in such a short period of time required an expensive and complicated double-entry visa, which involved a trip to London to have our fingerprints taken. We also needed a much more easily obtained Mongolian visa. Our flights went via Moscow, which seemed straightforward, but were with different airlines. This meant that we needed to check-in our bikes (that were packed into large cardboard boxes) in both Manchester and Moscow. It was very difficult to work out what the various airlines' bike policies were, so we risked hefty oversized baggage charges. We also had to navigate our way to the Mongolian border from Barnaul Airport, which was the closest we could get to the western border crossing. Although this distance looked unsubstantial on a map compared to the vast size of Russia, it was in fact about 800 kilometres with no guaranteed public transport. We intended to look for a bus or possibly to hitch a lift and would work it out when we got into Russia.

The journey went pretty well in the end. The Manchester to Moscow flight via Brussels worked well despite a quick connection and the bikes were a very reasonable 45 euros each to transport. In Moscow Airport, we sampled some excellent Russian food and observed two Russian women having a fight in a restaurant; it appeared that one had tried to steal from the other. We were able to check our bikes in with a reasonable service charge and boarded the plane to Barnaul in good time. From Barnaul, we quickly found a taxi which took us about 200 kilometres to the town of Gorno Altaysk in the Altai mountains. The journey was interesting in itself, since neither of us had been to Russia before and the first experience of any new country is always fascinating. Russia's past success during Soviet days was illustrated by the large number of high-rise buildings, factories and other infrastructure. Many of these buildings now looked shabby and in disrepair, although Russia was far more developed than either of us had expected. The roads were in great condition and smooth tarmac guided us away from the sprawling city of Barnaul, and into the Altai mountains. Stopping for fuel, we were amazed at how cheap the petrol was; less than a third of what it costs at home in the UK. Perhaps this is not surprising when considering Russia's domination of the oil market.

After a few hours we were deposited at the bus station in Gorno Altaysk, a large town set in forested mountains that seemed to act as a transport hub for the surrounding region. After waiting for an hour at the bus station it seemed that we were not going to be able to find a bus to take us to Kosh Agach; the last town before the Mongolian border. We appeared to be stuck, so were about to start assembling the bikes to cycle to the main road and attempt to hitch a lift. This was obviously a risky and uncertain strategy that neither of us thought was ideal. Luckily at that stage, we bumped into a Russian cyclist who had been touring around the Altai Mountains for the previous couple of weeks. He was friendly, helpful and delighted that we were travelling through his country. He went over to a group of taxi drivers and found somebody heading our way with a local family. He agreed to take us the 600-kilometre distance to Kosh Agach, for the equivalent of 30 pounds each, a ridiculously good deal in our opinion. It is amazing how easily problems tend to be sorted out when travelling. Soon we were loading our bags into a rickety old taxi, strapping our bike boxes onto its roof, then driving around Gorno Altaysk, looking for one particular flat in a concrete jungle of Soviet apartment blocks. Eventually, our driver found the family he was looking for. A man and his young daughter said an emotional goodbye to a lady who was staying at home, before getting into the taxi for the long journey.

The eight-hour car journey along the famous Chuysky Trakt road that cuts through the massive Altai Mountain range was spectacular and would have been worth the trip on its own. The quality of the road was excellent, although would not have been high on my list for cycle touring due to the fast-moving traffic and lack of space on the roadside. The road followed a fast-flowing river on which rafting was a popular pastime. It was initially quite touristy, with many hotels and restaurants and a lot of traffic from Russians visiting the area. This was soon left behind though, giving way to wide plains, mountain passes, open grasslands and herds of wild horses. The varied landscapes continued as we left the mountains behind and entered a barren wilderness, with no vegetation or rivers in sight. We were now in a desert and approaching our destination. Kosh Agach, means *the last tree* and is aptly named! It is a very odd place that was much bigger than we had expected with good local amenities, but it had a forgotten, decaying feel to it. We were dropped off at a hotel, where we paid an extremely drunk lady for one night in a foul-smelling room. A quick visit to a shop where we met lots more extremely drunk people, persuaded us that it was not a town to explore that night. We bought some noodles from the shop and hid in our hotel. We built the bikes, loaded them up and got an early night ready for the final part of our journey to the border the next day. It was at that point that I realised that I didn't have my helmet. It must have fallen out of the taxi when we opened the door to drop off the girl and her father a few hundred kilometres back along the road. This was a blow since I didn't expect to be able to buy a bike helmet any time soon. I would have to be careful.

An early start the next morning meant that we were cycling our fatbikes by half past seven. They were working brilliantly and had survived the flight well. Just outside the hotel we met a Polish motorcyclist who unfortunately had an issue with her visa and was concerned that she wouldn't be able to cross the border with her Russian friends. She gave us some useful information about the two most common routes across Mongolia, including that the more southerly route was currently being paved. We were hoping to hitch a ride along the road between Kosh Agach and Mongolia, a distance of around 60 kilometres. Riding around town though, we couldn't find anybody with a large enough vehicle to help us out. After around 20 minutes of fruitless searching we decided to start riding. Either we would find a lift on the way or we would ride the distance ourselves. The latter option was not ideal since the riding was dull; along a completely flat, straight tarmac road and into a roaring headwind. After around 20 kilometres we were both feeling demoralised and tired since we had not planned to cycle this leg of the journey. It was costing us valuable time that we could have been spending in Mongolia.

Then our luck changed. We were offered a lift by two Russian families on the way to Mongolia for an off-road driving adventure. They helped us to strap our bikes onto the roof of the two vehicles they were driving. Each of us got into one and we were moving once more. They were a friendly bunch and within 40 minutes we were at the Tashanta border crossing. Mongolia was now only a few kilometres away. We stocked up on food at one of the many shops by the border, waved goodbye to the friendly families and cycled towards the Russian border checkpoint. Two Russian border guards waved us past the queue of cars and trucks. Soon afterwards, we were let through the barrier to have our passports stamped. One more barrier was opened for us before we entered no-man's land and the *start point* of our fatbiking adventure.

Day 1: Into to the land of the nomads

Distance travelled: 79.48 km

Man's joy is in wide-open spaces
- Mongolian proverb

Thanking the extremely friendly Russian border guards, we began the 20-kilometre ride across no-man's land between the two border posts. The tarmac road climbed gradually up to the pass that was separating us from Mongolia. We were finally approaching the country I had dreamt about cycling through for most of the last decade. It was windy and chilly under the mid-morning overcast sky, but whenever the sunlight broke through a gap in the clouds, it instantly became much warmer. We were alone on the road for most of the 90-or-so minutes that it took us to ride between the borders, but now and again groups of cars that had been let through one of the two borders passed us in convoy.

Situated between the two border posts was a gate between barbed wire fences, guarded by an extremely excitable Mongolian soldier who appeared to have an extremely lonely job. We approached on our fatbikes, which he was very interested to inspect and began animatedly shouting at us in broken English. Suddenly he screamed "*bus*" as a very full coach that had come all the way from the capital city of Kazakhstan approached. It turned out that this bus only travels once a week between Astana and the Mongolian city of Olgii, via Barnaul. The route was advertised on the bus windscreen in Cyrillic text; Астана - Барнаул - Олгии. When the bus pulled up at the border post, the smiling guard disappeared instantly without saying goodbye; our first experience of the Mongolian habit of leaving without any comment, gesture or warning. Waiting for a few minutes we sheltered from the wind in the lee of the large bus, while he boarded it, carried out whatever duties he decided were required, before dismounting, opening the gate and waving us through.

I suspected that we may then have been crossing the official land border between the two countries, whose relative development was comically illustrated as the gate marked the end of the perfect asphalt and the beginning of a sandy dirt track. We expected to be riding on similar tracks for most of our adventure. A strong tailwind blew us up the final pass before the Mongolian border post, then a stunningly beautiful descent through the mountainous, barren steppe began. To the south were the largest of the Altai Mountains, sitting in the far west of Mongolia with their bright white snow-capped peaks and glistening glaciers in front of the

9

clear blue sky that lay behind them. Having left the smooth tarmac road surface behind, we let some air out of our giant tyres to allow them to cushion the bumpy road surface and make for a smoother ride. The large, spongy wheels absorbed all but the largest bumps and turned what would have been difficult riding on a loose surface into a formality.

Soon we could see a surprisingly modern looking border crossing, through which we were waved by another guard who proceeded to offer us an appalling rate to exchange our US dollars into Mongolian tugrik, no doubt a regular service he offers tourists! Thanking him, we refused his offer, hoping to find a better rate in the border town of Tsagaanuur. Crossing the border was very easy, although the Kazakhs and Mongolians on the bus from Kazakhstan didn't seem to be as adept at queuing as we are in Britain. About ten people forced past us at passport control, quickly teaching us that we would need to physically push against others to keep our place in the line. From then on, we held our own and fortunately didn't end up behind the entire busload of travellers from Kazakhstan, who arrived at the border post just after us. A short time later our passports were stamped, and we were allowed to pass into Mongolia at last. We had entered the westernmost Aimag (administrative region) of Mongolia, named *Bayan-Ölgii.*

Our first stop was the border town of Ulaanbaishint. Straight away our conversation turned to food. We needed to plan what supplies were required for the next couple of days. First though, we needed to sample Mongolian *buuz* for the first time. Buuz are steamed dumplings filled with mutton, onions and garlic, and are a staple of the Mongolian diet. Finding a roadside café, we entered to the silent stare of its ten-or-so occupants. Soon though, they started chatting again and we were offered a seat at the end of a long table. I squeezed onto a bench and a young lady moved up a seat to share one with a friend sitting next to her, making room for Phil. The table's occupants looked at us expectantly. Pointing to the buuz on the table next to us, we managed to order six dumplings each, along with some milky tea, known as *Suutei Tsai.* Inside the adjacent the kitchen, three giggling teenage girls made fresh dough, rolled it out, cut it into individual dumplings and stuffed each with mutton. They then steamed them over a boiling pot sitting on a large cast iron stove.

Meanwhile, we tried to exchange some US dollars for Mongolian tugrik. During my round the world trip, I cycled through Uzbekistan, Kazakhstan, Tajikistan and Kyrgyzstan. In these countries, I found it very easy to exchange dollars for the local currency in each town that I passed through. People were desperate to exchange their money for the much more stable dollar, often offering better rates than banks. Here though, it seemed that people weren't as ready to part with the local currency. Perhaps the tugrik holds its value better than the currency of the Central Asian countries, or perhaps Mongolians don't use money as often. The nomadic lifestyle is all but self-sufficient, so I supposed that dollars were pretty useless in this remote town in the undeveloped west of the country. Fortunately for us, the border guard who had offered us tugrik at the border entered the café and we managed to negotiate a better rate, 1700 tugrik for 1 dollar (although the official rate was around 2050). We exchanged 40 dollars; enough to get us to a town with a bank in a couple of days' time.

Our food arrived and two of the table's occupants passed us ketchup and a black sauce, which was similar to soy, along with a large flask of *tsai.* The flask was undoubtedly a Chinese import, with a picture of a trumpet above the golden italic phrase; *the sound of music, lucky bird.* Most of the people on the table looked Kazakh, with angular features, beaked noses and high cheek bones, although one man had the rounder, more gentle face of a Mongolian. The Bayan-Olgii Aimig is mainly inhabited by Kazakhs, whose numbers increased threefold during Soviet days. When the Soviet Union broke up in 1991, Mongolia became a democracy and many Kazakhs moved back to their homeland for a better life, leading to a significant drop in population. Many have since returned though, and the population is again on the up. The people sitting on our table were wearing western-style clothes and were generally a very friendly bunch. Suddenly, they decided it was time to leave. Again, they disappeared without any formal farewell.

Phil and I looked at our map, deciding which way we would go. Paper maps of Mongolia had been difficult to get hold of. I had purchased two, both of which were very large scale, the more detailed being 1: 1,600,000. This scale was impossible to directly navigate from, but the map included names of almost all of the towns, which was useful when asking for directions and to plan an overall route. Having spoken to various people, including the Polish motorcyclist in Kosh-Agach and the Russians who gave us a lift to the border, it seemed that most of the road traffic heading east across the country would take the more developed, southerly route. Having come to Mongolia to experience its endless, unpopulated wilderness, we decided to take the more remote northern route. It would take us over mountain ranges, across a branch of the Gobi Desert, around two large and famously beautiful lakes, and then through vast areas of grassland for a few days, before reaching the more populated central regions of the country. Looking at our map, we could see that we would visit a couple of small towns the following day, so we would not need to carry many supplies. We purchased a few bottles of water and snacks from a little shop, to go with what we had bought in the Russian border town of Tashanta.

Cycling out of Ulaanbaishint, we were instantly surrounded by the epic vastness of the Mongolian countryside. A tailwind blew us along a slightly downhill dirt track in the centre of a wide plain between two large ranges of hills. The steppe was stony and sandy, but fertile enough to be covered in short grass, It was dotted in *gers;* the traditional Mongolian round, canvas dwelling, more commonly known as *yurts* in most other countries. Large herds of goats and sheep grazed on either side of the road and horses stood close to many of the gers. Other than the track and a line of telegraph poles, the landscape was completely untouched by any permanent influence from man. Rounding a corner, we passed a large, deep-blue lake, surrounded by many more gleaming white gers. On its shoreline, were large herds of grazing animals, in front of a backdrop of grass-covered hills.

Soon we reached Tsagaanuur, a relatively large town that contained a few permanent buildings, an empty school and a few dozen gers. Kids played in large groups and rode cheap Chinese bikes around in circles until we approached, at which point they came over to race us, accelerating as they passed by. This competitive need to race is a habit that all children seem to have and I have experienced it in every country through which I have cycled. I sometimes took part in the "race", overtaking the children, then letting them pass me before waving after them. Reaching the centre of the town, we stopped at a shop and were instantly surrounded. Soon the kids were all having a go on our fatbikes and were, quite incredibly, able to ride them with all the heavy bags attached even though they were far too big for them. Kids in Mongolia learn to ride horses from a very early age so have excellent balance and we thought that this would have probably helped their bike riding skills. As we left the shop, a motorcyclist approached and asked us if we wanted tsai (tea). Nodding, we followed him on his motorbike as he led us for around a kilometre to his ger, on the outskirts of the town.

After arriving, we introduced ourselves before he told us his name was Batbayar. Batbayar's family ger sat on a patch of stony ground surrounded by grass. We were introduced to the head of the family, an elderly gentleman with a friendly face and a large moustache. He wore a shirt, cardigan, and a waistcoat jacket as well as a flat cap on his head. He gestured for us to enter the ger, which had a beautiful interior. The wooden trellis walls were lined in colourful felt blankets and the roof made from around 100 willow sticks, like bike wheel spokes, supporting the white felt material that covers the ger. Directly above us was the *toono*, the roof ring, which is the most complex part of the structure, being perfectly circular w th slots cut to hold each of the roof struts in place. Around the ger were seven beds, a sofa, a table and chairs, an area where meat was hung behind a patterned green sheet, a kitchen area and a cupboard containing tools, horse riding equipment and other possessions. In the centre sat a large cast iron stove, next to which crouched Batbayar 's mother who was preparing food for us. Soon a plate of bread and cheese sat in front of us next to a steaming bowl of milky tsai. Then came a bowl of rice with mutton, along with more tsai. The food was all delicious and very filling; excellent fuel for fatbiking.

As we ate, I explained that I had lost my helmet in Russia and that I needed to buy a hat to protect myself from the sun. I assumed that there was no chance I would be able to buy another helmet in any of the small towns in the west of the country. Batbayar offered to sell me his cap for the equivalent of three dollars, which I agreed to, and the problem was solved. It soon became clear that the family expected money for the food, which we were perfectly happy to part with since it cost very little and they had been very friendly. This was something we would bear in mind for the rest of our trip though, since it can be damaging if locals start thinking of tourists as a source of money, leading to the loss of aspects of traditional lifestyles. I have been to many communities around the world where tourism has led to people no longer pursuing typical jobs, but making money by selling goods or services to tourists, sometimes at grossly inflated prices. This was not yet a problem in this part of Mongolia, since there are so few tourists passing through.

It turned out to be the only time that a Mongolian family asked for money for hospitality inside a ger. As we left, we were given a bag of curd, a hard snack made from fermented milk, with a salty, cheesy taste. I thought it was delicious, whereas Phil thought it was the most disgusting thing he had ever eaten. In the days of Genghis Khan, a network of horse-mounted messengers was created to quickly carry the Khan's orders from one side of his empire to the other. It is said that these messengers could travel over 100 kilometres in a day and could continue for ten days eating nothing but curd! The experience was a great insight into the life of Batbayar's family. We were both very keen to meet some *real* nomads living out in the steppe that lay ahead.

Waving farewell, we left Tsagaanuur in the late afternoon and soon approached another lake that was glimmering in the low evening sunlight. On the shore, was the silhouette of what could only have been cycle tourists. This was confirmed when they walked over to chat to us. The friendly German couple were on a much longer trip than us, but had found their crossing of Mongolia very hard work. They were both very tired and keen to get into Russia the following day. They reported that the terrain had been very difficult, and they were both sick of mosquitoes but thought we would enjoy the route much more on our fatbikes. They told us that they had spent two half-days pushing through the desert near Uvs Nuur, a giant saline lake we would pass in a few days. They had also taken a 100-kilometre detour around nearby Achit Nuur (another large lake), because a bridge over the Khatuugin Gol had collapsed. *Nuur* and *gol* are Mongolian words for lake and river respectively. This was potentially a big problem for us too. It would delay us by over a day if we had to cycle around Achit Nuur. After passing on our experience of Mongolia so far, particularly of the border crossing to Russia, we cycled on, planning to ride for another hour-or-so before we stopped for the night.

The road, which was now little more than a jeep track, closely followed a river at the bottom of a large valley. A few gers were situated on the grass near the river, next to which were more large herds of sheep and goats, sometimes consisting of over 100 animals. The sheep seemed to get on fine with the goats in the mixed herds containing animals of both genders and all ages. After our long journey to Mongolia, we fancied a quiet campsite that night, so we passed the gers before finding a spot of our own by the riverside, out of sight and quiet. While pitching my tent, I stopped to think about where I was; in the remote west of perhaps the greatest remaining wilderness in the world. Two days ago, I was still in Sheffield having just finished a very busy first year working as a physics teacher. Now I was camping in a Mongolian valley; my biggest worry being how much food and water we would need to carry and which way we needed to go. I love cycle touring!

Soon our camp was set up and we were eating dinner, the highlight of which was a tasty salami-like sausage we had bought in Russia. A Kazakh motorcyclist suddenly appeared, heading our way. We were confused as to where he was going, until he wobbled between the stones and grassy tussocks that lay between the road and our tents, approaching our camp. It was clear that he was curious about who we were and wanted to say hello. He was a young man, wearing western-style clothes and on his way to Tsagaanuur to drink vodka with his friends. After showing him our bikes, tents and many of our possessions, we offered him some biscuits, which he quickly ate. He stayed for around 20 minutes, then disappeared instantly. We thought he must have come from a ger further down the valley and hoped that he wouldn't visit us again later with his vodka-drinking friends! A few dry bushes provided us with enough fuel to make a small fire, using the twigs that had dropped onto the floor. We managed to heat up a pan of water to make tea, which was an unexpected luxury as we had not been able to buy any petrol in Tsagaanuur for Phil's stove. Both absolutely shattered, we went to bed before sunset, at around half past nine. I lay in bed very content with life and drifted off to sleep almost instantly, despite my foam sleeping mat being very thin and not at all comfortable.

Our first view of the Mongolian Steppe

The lake near Tsagaanuur

Batbayar (centre) with his friend and me in their family ger

Phil with the man of the house

Day 2: The swamp
Distance travelled: 78.13 kilometres

Don't undo your bootlaces until you have seen the river.
- Mongolian proverb

With a few aches and pains, I awoke at sunrise. Shortly afterwards my alarm went off and woke Phil up too. After a quick breakfast we packed up our campsite and loaded up the bikes. During our trip it usually took a bit over an hour for us to get going in the morning with time for a leisurely breakfast and a hot drink. The ride day began along the riverside, a few hundred metres away from the jeep track that was higher up the valley side. We headed towards four gers for around 15 minutes crossing grassy and rocky terrain in a deep valley. The gers were built on the edge of the river in a wide part of the valley, which was a beautifully scenic place for their inhabitants to choose to settle for the season. The riding was fun and relatively easy on the fatbikes, which were more than capable of riding over the very bumpy *shortcut* that we were taking back to the track. Soon we made it to the "*main road*", to waves and incredulous looks from the nomads standing by their gers.

The track continued to follow the river downhill for around another ten kilometres, until the mountain range came to an end and we were spat out into a vast plain that stretched so far to the north and south that we couldn't see where it ended. To the south was Achit Nuur; the giant but shallow freshwater lake that the Germans had had to cycle around to avoid fording the Khatuugin Gol. To the east, which was the direction in which we were heading, we could make out the town of Nogoonuur on our side of the river. Around ten kilometres beyond this was another town named *Bukmurin*. Past Bukmurin lay another large mountain range that we would be crossing at some point during the next couple of days. When we would cross it depended very much on whether we could get through the river that lay ahead. Between the two towns lay a large expanse of deep green vegetation in which the river widened before entering Achit Nuur. We decided to attempt to cross the river between the two towns to save ourselves the long detour around the lake. We hoped that crossing the river close to Achit Nuur's northern shore would be easier than doing so further away from the lake, since the river split into lots of smaller channels forming a delta of sorts. Our thinking was that the river would be shallower with less current that the single main channel, although we had absolutely no idea if the crossing was possible... we would soon see.

18

The downhill gradient continued, but became less steep as the plain neared the river. The temperature increased as the morning progressed, and our altitude decreased. As the air grew hotter and more humid, the number of flying insects increased rapidly. When camping the previous night, we had both been bitten a few times by mosquitoes, but there were not many and we kept them at bay with insect repellent. Here, not only were there millions of mosquitoes, there were giant horseflies that bit us as soon as they made contact with our skin. These bites were very painful and felt similar to a wasp sting. At the speed we were cycling downhill the mosquitoes couldn't *dock* onto our skin to bite us but the horseflies could. Cycling as fast as we could to try to prevent bites, we soon reached the settlement of Nogoonuur.

Having expected little more than a few gers and possibly a small shop we were surprised to find a large town, although it appeared to be completely deserted. When cycling into the settlement we didn't see anybody for around five minutes. All of the doors were shut and the place felt like a post-apocalyptic ghost town. Speculating about the reasons for this we thought that perhaps it had been abandoned after the breakup of the Soviet Union, or perhaps that people lived there in the winter and in gers during the summer. Stopping to consider our options we were soon covered in mosquitoes. Perhaps this was the reason that nobody was outside.

After coating ourselves in *deet*, which is an effective but apparently carcinogenic insect repellent that can damage waterproof clothing, the relentless mosquito onslaught subsided slightly. This allowed us to continue exploring the town in slightly less discomfort. Eventually we came across three middle-aged men in a compound of ramshackle buildings. They were mechanics and were fixing an ancient looking tractor as we approached. They seemed to be entirely unconcerned by the mosquitoes and completely unsurprised to see us. I asked if there was a *magazin* (shop in Russian) in town, to which they nodded and the nearest grabbed his motorbike, beckoning for us to follow. Many Mongolians are able to speak Russian well; a result of close ties with the former Soviet Union. He led us into the town "*centre*", which consisted of several large buildings including what looked like a town hall and a deserted school. Passing a petrol station, we filled up our fuel bottle with unleaded, which we would use to power Phil's stove, before finding the shop. It was little more than a cupboard full of out-of-date tinned food, noodles and vodka. I saw a bottle of coke with a sell-by-date of January 2003 on display! Despite encouragement from our now growing audience, I opted against buying a litre bottle of vodka that was cheaper than the mineral water in the shop and instead bought eight litres of water, four packets of noodles, some ropey-looking potatoes, a can of pasta sauce and a packet of *choco pies*, which are a sort of marshmallowy chocolate snack from China that is available across most of Asia. Despite their rather bland taste and stale texture, experience has taught me that choco pies are one of the better options in such shops.

I left the shop to find Phil surrounded by a larger crowd than before, most of whom were very drunk even though it was well before noon. The nomads we had seen so far did not appear to drink much but there seemed to be serious drinking problems amongst the men who lived in towns. They were not aggressive or unkind and seemed eager to help despite the stench of vodka on their breath and their unkempt, dirty appearance. I felt very sorry for them as I thought about their lot in life. They live in a town that is unimaginably cold for over six months of the year and that is infested with mosquitoes for most of the rest. There are no employment prospects and it would be impossible for them to purchase animals to start up a traditional nomadic lifestyle without any capital. Perhaps many of them had been nomadic but had lost their herds during a bad winter. A severe winter in Mongolia is known as a *zud*, during which large numbers of livestock die as there is no food for them to graze on because there is so much snow that they cannot get to the vegetation underneath. Harsh zuds can lead to economic crises and widespread food shortages throughout the country and are becoming increasingly common with climate change.

We asked the tractor mechanic about crossing the river to Bukmurin. He seemed positive about our chances signalling that the water would be no be deeper than our waists but quite fast flowing. Many of the other men were not so positive, telling us that the river would be over our heads if we tried to cross it and that we should go around Achit Nuur instead. Given that the tractor mechanic was the only sober male in the group we decided to trust him and risk the river crossing. Finding some shade from the heat of the sun we put on more insect repellent, ate some choco pies, then set off towards the river. Soon we had entered a giant waterlogged swamp across which ran a flooded jeep track. There was no point trying to follow the track so instead we followed a compass bearing that would lead us to Bukmurin where we expected to be able to join the main road once more. The mosquitoes and horse flies soon became completely unbearable. We were constantly swatting the buzzing insects when cycling, but were instantly covered whenever we had to stop. It is hard to explain quite how horrific the experience was! When stationary, at least twenty of the blood-sucking demons had bitten us within ten seconds. Large red bites were appearing all over both of us and every now and then, to vary the torture, a horsefly contributed to the pain. Despite this we were progressing well and were successfully crossing the swamp. We were taking a path that normal bikes would have had no chance of passing since the ground was so soft and squashy.

Our first major obstacle was a small river channel, knee deep and slow-flowing. We easily lifted our bikes through and continued into thicker vegetation where shrubs had grown higher than head height. As we approached the first major river channel the intensity of the mosquitoes seemed to increase, if that was possible. Weaving through large bushes we eventually reached the river and my heart sank; it was over ten metres wide and had a visibly strong current that would be very difficult to wade through. Lying the bikes down on the stony ground we walked to the river, which I instantly jumped into to wash off the mosquitoes and give myself a few seconds of respite. To our delight we were able to walk across the river that was much shallower than it looked. The tractor mechanic was right; it only reached our waists. One at a time we lifted our bikes across the water, crossing the channel trouble free (although receiving another hundred-or-so bites in the process). Continuing for another 20 minutes through this hell-on-earth, we eventually reached the second channel that was larger than the first, but at this point there was absolutely zero chance that we were turning back. We reached the river at a bend, which wasn't the best point to cross because the current was much stronger and the river much deeper. After about five minutes of pushing our bikes along the riverbank we found a straight part of the river, which was possible to ford. As it was deeper than the last channel the two of us carried one bike at a time at head-height since the water was above our hips. Soon we were across and battling on to the town that we could now see only a few hundred metres away, underneath ten-or-so circling birds-of-prey.

Eventually we reached the town with swollen faces, itchy limbs and depleted energy levels but we had made it! We had saved a day of riding around the lake and would soon be back into the mountains. Finding a shop in the much more welcoming and populated town of Bukmurin, we were able to shelter from the insect onslaught and refuel on coke. Soon afterwards we left the shop to find that the weather had dramatically changed from bright sunshine to thick cloud and a strong wind, threatening an incoming storm. A large patch of heavy rain was approaching across the swamp, which we could see from a long way away due to the flatness of the landscape. The wind was blowing from the west, which was good news since it would soon aid us when cycling along the road leading east. More importantly though, the mosquitoes had disappeared, clearly unable to fly in the strong wind. Feeling much more positive, Phil went into a bank in his lycra shorts where he planned to exchange some money. Apparently, the locals weren't too impressed with his choice of outfit and he wasn't sure if they refused to serve him or whether they didn't offer an exchange service. He suspected the latter! We continued out of the town, still with enough money to make it to the next town and feeling very pleased with ourselves for managing to cross the river and passing the swamp.

Just after the leaving the pleasant town we reached a spectacular outcrop of red sandstone crags that were around 50 metres high. More hawks circled overhead, peering down on their territory below and looking for prey. Finding a comfortable rock to sit on we stopped for lunch, taking in the beautiful setting. To the south was the swamp we had just crossed and to the north was another large grassy plain in front of the mountains that we hoped to reach that evening.

After lunch a short climb over a small pass led us to a descent onto the wide plain. Although beautiful, the repetitive views were now playing mind-games with my head and the mountains on the far side of the plain looked a very long way away. The steppe didn't change much but unfortunately the wind direction had changed, meaning that we were now cycling into a strong headwind that limited our speed to about ten kilometres-per-hour. The flat and featureless landscape was thirty kilometres wide and took all afternoon to cross. Every time I raised my weary head to look at the horizon in hope that we were nearly there, the mountains didn't seem to be getting any closer. It was incredibly demoralising and psychologically challenging after the horrific experience in the swamp. Eventually though, we made it and climbed a few hundred metres into the mountains to escape from the mosquitoes that had returned when the sun came out again. Our tactic didn't work so we had the immense pleasure of blood-sucking company while eating dinner that evening; potatoes with surprisingly delicious canned Russian pasta sauce. After dinner, I entered my mosquito free tent and was so tired that I fell asleep with pen in hand after writing just a single line in my diary.

Crossing the plain before reaching Nogoonuur

The road to Nogoonuur, with Achit Nuur visible on the horizon

The swamp between Nogoonuur and Bukmurin

I thought we'd never get across this branch of the Bukmurin Gol

Harder than it looks!

Infinite horizons, riding against the wind

Day 3: Mountain passes and Üüreg Nuur
Distance travelled: 77.29 kilometres

If you drink the water from a place, then also follow the custom of that place
- Mongolian proverb

After waking at around seven o'clock, we used most of our remaining water to make a pan full of tea and another full of noodles. Knowing that there was a large lake that contained potable water a few kilometres away, we weren't worried about running out of water to drink. The ride to the top of the pass in the cool morning air was beautiful as we climbed on a smooth dirt track that wound up the grassy mountainside between high rocky peaks. Soon we reached higher land where the ground became less dry and more fertile, allowing thicker and longer grass to grow. Over the top of the pass was a wide pasture spreading out in front of us and surrounded by mountains. With the longer grass came nomadic families living in gers, dotted across the landscape and surrounded by grazing herds. Around 20 children played outside the gers, some of whom had bikes and were whizzing around in circles. When they spotted us they waved enthusiastically, which we returned to their delight. Throughout our crossing of Mongolia, we met hundreds of nomadic children because they were all on their summer holiday. Mongolian children are at school for most the year where they board during the freezing winter months, giving them access to a reliable water supply, sanitation and warmth, as well a good education. Eight years of school attendance is compulsory in Mongolia and educating their children is now a priority for Mongolian parents. This has led to the remarkable achievement of a 98 percent literacy rate throughout the country.

As we approached one of the gers a man came over on his motorbike to say hello, before admiring our fatbikes. He had a ride on mine and seemed to very much enjoy himself since he returned with a large smile spreading from ear-to-ear revealing a mouthful of tobacco-stained teeth. He saw our nearly empty water bottles and motioned for us to wait while he went to fill them up. Taking the bottles, he sped off back to his home. He returned a few minutes later with our bottles full of slightly brown water, along with another family member who also wanted to look at our bikes. What a kind thing to do! Without us asking or making a signal he had realised that we were short of water so solved our problem. Phil gave him some cigarette filter papers he had brought to give away as presents, on advice from a guidebook. The man looked at them confused before working out what they were, motioning rolling a cigarette. He then took one out of the packet and proceeded to chew the paper, before spitting it out and nodding happily. We weren't sure how pleased he was with his present!

Climbing on, we soon reached the highest pass of the mountain range at 2020 metres. At the top a spectacular view over the next landscape was revealed. A shimmering, giant and dark-blue lake lay in front of us surrounded by grassy steppe and many more rocky mountain ranges in all directions. Our track headed in a straight line down the mountainside, rounding the bottom of the lake then climbing up a mountain slope on the other side of the plain. Large herds of horses stood close to the track as we descended quickly to the beautiful *Üüreg Nuur*, which is an endorheic lake, meaning it has no outflow. It is one of the smaller lakes in this area of Mongolia, known as the Great Lakes Depression, despite it being 20 kilometres by 18 kilometres in size. It has the reputation of being the most beautiful of the Mongolian Great Lakes due to its spectacular surroundings. It is also apparently excellent for fishing, containing salmon and the legendary Mongolian Taimen, which can reach two metres in length and have a mass of up to 100 kilograms.

Descending quickly we soon reached the southern shore of the lake, which was mercifully mosquito-free as there was a strong wind blowing. The constant breeze created small waves that broke onto the pebbly beach lining the edge of the water. We were soon swimming in the surprisingly warm lake, which was wonderfully refreshing as we hadn't washed since the evening before crossing the mosquito-infested swamp. After cleaning ourselves with biodegradable soap, we washed our cycling clothes before sitting on the beach to eat lunch. We relaxed on the lakeside until the wind-speed dropped and the mosquitoes returned.

Before leaving, we filled our water bottles with the potable, but very slightly saline lake water then continued across the plain, passing many more large herds of sheep and goats as well as an empty-looking tourist ger camp. The climb up the pass on the east side of the lake provided spectacular views back over Üüreg Nuur. At the top was another high grassy pasture on which large herds of beautiful wild horses lived. What struck me most about these incredible animals was how lean and muscular they were, smaller and skinnier that their British cousins. Their speed, as they galloped across the grasslands, was impressive but their stamina more so. They seemed to be able to run forever. The bumpy track that crossed the plain seemed to have claimed quite a few mechanical victims over the years since it was scattered with broken car parts. We came across a broken-down minibus, outside which a group of teenagers calmly awaited rescue. The constant bumping had affected Phil's pannier rack setup by causing it to move slightly, meaning that the bottom of the rack was in contact with the rear derailleur. Fifteen minutes of filing a bracket that the mount was attached to provide a bit more clearance to the derailleur that may have otherwise been damaged.

After twenty kilometres we had crossed the mountain range and reached yet another wonderful viewpoint looking over another vast hilly landscape, on which lived hundreds of nomads, and with another large lake to the north. Deciding that this vantage point would make for a memorable campsite, we left the road at the top of a very steep slope. A car was struggling to drive uphill, revving loudly and trying to weave its way up; its wheels spinning and clutch slipping. Rounding a small mound on the roadside we found a relatively flat piece of the hillside where we pitched our tents with a panoramic view of the stunning, typically Mongolian scenery in all directions. We set up camp, made dinner and caught up on our diaries. The sky was slowly turning a vivid red as the sun disappeared behind the mountains. The sunset was one of the most beautiful I have ever seen.

Almost ready for bed, we heard the quiet whirring of a distant motorcycle that appeared to be heading towards us. Soon enough it became clear that the rider was heading our way. A few minutes later he and his son dismounted and came to greet us. The man sat down and smiled. He had a go on Phil's bike which he loved, then started rifling through our possessions. He was so interested in what we had. I assumed that he had never seen a petrol stove, a Swiss army knife, a fold up pan, a cycling tool kit, a pannier, a compact tent, a blow-up mattress or (certainly) two fat bikes! He passed some of our kit to his son to have a look at. I grabbed a map to show him where we had been as well as our planned route, although I don't think he knew the geography of his country very well because he looked confused. We communicated to him that we had no petrol and wanted to make tea. He disconnected the fuel pipe from his motorbike, filled up our petrol bottle then reconnected it: problem solved! Lighting the stove, Phil made a pan of tea, which was slightly salty as it was made from the lake water. Pouring out two mugs of tea, Phil and I shared one and the man and his son the other. Suddenly they got up and hopped on their motorbike evidently deciding it was time to leave. Phil gave the man a couple of fishing hooks, which he was delighted with, signalling towards Üüreg Nuur. Waving as he left, Phil and I looked at each other and laughed at the fact that he had just searched through our equipment without asking and moved around like a whirlwind through our campsite! He was lovely though; this wasn't rude behaviour, just different from what we are used to. On that note we went to bed, both having fallen in love with this wonderful country.

A beautiful track into the hills

Üüreg Nuur

Wild horses

The climb from Üüreg Nuur

Night-time visit

What a sky!

Day 4: To Ulaangom
Distance travelled: 62 kilometres

'We sat on the snow and looked at the country far below us... we nibbled Kendal Mint Cake.'
- Sir Edmund Hillary on the first successful ascent of Everest

Our food supplies were low and our only water was briny, from Üüreg Nuur. Having exclusively drunk this water for most of the previous day, we were getting rather sick of its taste. Due to the salt dissolved in it, I couldn't prevent my mouth from drying out no matter how much of it I drank. I put a green tea bag into each of our water bottles to attempt to mask the taste of the salt mixed with the iodine we had used to purify the water. This worked quite well, making the disgusting water slightly less so. Our breakfast was equally awful, consisting of salty dried noodles and even more salty soup. Entirely sick of the salt overload, we couldn't wait to reach Ulaangom where we would be able to get a decent meal. Our guidebook even said that one of the restaurants there served steak!

After packing up our campsite we were ready to depart. We decided to descend straight down the hillside off-road to intersect the track at the bottom, rather than to head back up to the track. The ground wasn't too bumpy as we rode down the grassy, stony slope. Cycling directly towards the rising sun at around 30 kilometres per hour, we were soon onto the large plain in the centre of a bowl of mountains. The fatbikes took the descent in their stride, absorbing all of the small bumps and making it easy to ride on the difficult terrain. Soon we reached the main track that bisected the vast grassy pastures, which we needed to cross before the final climb of the day. On the plain we saw a nomad horse rider attempting to catch a wild horse with a lasso. He galloped around it and threw the lasso at the horse until he managed to position the rope over its head, then led it struggling back to his ger. He would probably attempt to train it to add to his herd.

Having crossed the plain, a breath-taking eight-kilometre climb up the far side of the bowl was sapping our energy as we struggled against a headwind. We were both finding the riding very difficult on our limited food supplies, until I remembered that I had a secret stash of Kendal Mint Cake. The sugary, minty snack gave us an instant energy boost that transformed our mood and the final few kilometres of the climb seemed a lot easier. I could see why Kendal Mint Cake was the most popular food of the team on Sir Edmund Hillary's ascent of Everest and why Sir Ernest Shackleton took rations of it with him on his ill-fated Trans-Arctic

Expedition. As we neared the top of the climb, some of the largest mountains in Mongolia came into view to the south. Their towering rocky peaks were coated in snow above gigantic cliffs that peered down imperiously on the smaller grass-covered hills below.

Mountains have been revered in Mongolia since Genghis Khan's days. When he was young, he lost a battle against the *Merkit Tribe* and escaped death by hiding on *Burkhan Khaldun Mountain*. He pronounced the mountain sacred in response to the protection it offered him and spent three days there praying to the gods. At the peak of the mountain is the *Main Ovoo of Heaven,* a cairn-style pile of rocks that acts as site of worship for both Shamans and Buddhists, the two major traditional religions of Mongolia. All over Mongolia *Ovoos* are built at the top of mountains and on high mountain passes. They are worshipped during organised ceremonies, but it is also a custom to show your respect to the ovoo when travelling past. We reached the top of our mountain pass and sure enough, saw the ovoo covered in offerings including sweets, milk, curd, prayer flags and money. In exchange the Gods would provide a safe journey, pleasant weather and large livestock herds to those who paid their respects. We followed the tradition of circling the ovoo three times in a clockwise direction and throwing a rock onto the pile of rocks each time we completed a circuit. The mountain gods would hopefully be on our s de for the remainder of the journey.

A brilliant descent awaited us, leading from the pass to the vast desert that stretched out for hundreds of kilometres to the east. A narrow singletrack trail cut off the first corner of the main track but soon rejoined the wider, steeper and stonier trail. The descent led down a wide valley, which ended at the northern branch of the Gobi Desert. This vast desert stretches from our location in Mongolia to close to Beijing in China. Entering the Gobi marked the end of the mountainous region in the west of Mongolia. We would be crossing the most northern part of the desert for the next few days, but before attempting the crossing we would reach the capital of the *Uvs Aimag,* named *Ulaangom. Uvs* means grass in Mongolian, which is a slightly odd name for this part of the region since there was very little grass in sight. We would plan the logistics of surviving in this harsh landscape in Ulaangom that afternoon and evening.

While descending, we saw Uvs Nuur for the first time. Uvs Nuur is the largest lake in Mongolia with a vast surface area of 3,350 square kilometres. Incredibly, its average depth is just six metres, it has no outlet and its water is five times saltier than the sea. Despite its high salinity, it freezes from October to May every year.

The desert plain we were heading towards was formed by the enormous saline sea that once covered a much larger area but all that is left of it now is Uvs Nuur. The giant lake dominated the horizon to the northeast, so large that we couldn't make out its far side. At the bottom of the descent we entered a much drier, sandier landscape with far less vegetation than the endless alpine pastures that we had left behind us. All that could grow here were tough dry shrubs and sparse grasses. To our surprise, the road changed from a dirt track to a new tarmac road with a perfect surface.

We cruised along at 20 kilometres per hour and soon reached Ulaangom, crossing a few bridges over large rivers that flowed towards us from the mountains to the south, then on to Uvs Nuur to the north. Ulaangom seemed to be built on a more fertile piece of land, surrounded by a grassy area on which hundreds of gers were built. Presumably living close to the large city is very convenient for their inhabitants. On the way into the city almost every telegraph pole had a large hawk perched on top of it and many more circled around in the sky above us. We thought that these birds-of-prey probably scavenged food from the city. I reflected that this existence was somewhat different from the way that they had evolved to live. On the edge of the city was the first shop we had seen for a couple of days. I entered and purchased two cold bottles of Fanta, two Snickers and two ice creams. At this lower altitude with the powerful sun shining down on us, the temperature was far hotter than we had experienced so far. The refreshing snack was very welcome before we continued into the city centre. We found an excellent hotel in the north of the city, which had a garage to keep the bikes in, a warm shower and very surprisingly, relatively fast WiFi.

Ulaangom turned out to be a modern city, with wide tree-lined streets and large communist-style buildings built during the Soviet era. We found our way to the large *zakh* (market) in the north of the city, which had a large area containing food shops and stalls where we bought supplies for the desert crossing. I purchased two large bottles of Fanta which held more liquid that the water bottles I had on my bike. I would use these to carry water in the large bottle mounts on my bike's fork legs near the front wheel. I also had a three-litre water bladder that fit in my small rucksack, and room to strap one more water bottle onto the dry bag containing my tent, foam mat and sleeping bag, that was attached to my handlebars. This allowed me to carry a total of nine litres. At the market we found a fantastic restaurant where we had dumplings, eggs, mutton stew, noodles and rice all mixed together; a great lunch.

Back at the hotel, we planned the next part of our route using the WiFi. There were four main options: the most southerly route, which passed along the north side of another large lake named *Khyragas Nuur,* was probably the easiest option since we had heard that the surface had been partly paved; a route that climbed up to higher ground to the north of the Khan Khokhii Mountains sounded like the second easiest, being on a good track; the third and fourth options were two sandy tracks that crossed the desert close to Uvs Nuur, the northernmost of the two being a slightly longer route that followed the edge of the lake. Being on fatbikes we thought that it would be sacrilege to not try them out on the sandy desert tracks, as they are famously good for riding on sand. We decided to take the more southerly of these two routes that passed close to Uvs Nuur since we would then be able to see the lake without having to make a long detour up to its shore. We were using an incredibly good open-source map that was available for free download on the ViewRanger App; highly recommended for any travellers in Mongolia. It not only has all place names and roads marked, but also contour lines for the entire country showing the altitude at any point. We updated our maps to ensure we had the route near Uvs Nuur downloaded. It was important that we both carried paper maps too, in case of phone malfunction.

That evening we searched the local shops in vain for a Mongolian sim card to keep in touch with our wives, Laura (me) and Caroline (Phil). We were told that we had to go to the head office of the phone network (Mobicom) to get one from there in the morning. Returning to the hotel we went to the restaurant for the promised steak that I had read about in my guidebook. We both ordered one, to be told 15 minutes later that they had none. We then tried to order pork chops, but were then told again that they had none! Eventually we were told that they only had two things available on their long and varied menu: mutton dumplings and chicken with chips. Very disappointed, we ordered them instead. The restaurant in the hotel was very grand, with enough space for around 100 customers on large tables all laid for dinner. However, we were the only two there that night! Perhaps it was available for wedding receptions or other events, but I couldn't see how it would ever fill up otherwise. After a tasty local lager we headed up to bed, ready for an early start the following day.

Distant glaciers

Capturing a wild horse

Ovoo on top of the pass

Down to Ulaangom

Day 5: The Gobi Desert
Distance travelled: 93.15 kilometres

This desert is reported to be so long that it would take a year to go from end to end. And at the narrowest point it takes a month to cross it. It consists entirely of mountains and sands and valleys. There is nothing at all to eat.
- Marco Polo

Starting early we packed, showered, loaded our food and water onto the bikes and left the hotel, before heading into town. At a pharmacy we were surprised but pleased to find more sun cream, although it was very expensive, being largely a luxury item in Mongolia. At the mobile phone shop, we found a sim card, then bought some tasty pizza and large pieces of sponge cake from a small bakery. On the way out of the city we passed a large wrestling stadium with an impressive statue of a giant wrestler in the *devee* dance position, in which the wrestler imitates a falcon taking off. The wrestler in the statue was wearing the traditional outfit for that sport, which consists of long boots, an open fronted jacket with long sleeves and short silk trunks lined with leather. The reason for the open fronted jacket is fascinating. A long time ago during a national wrestling competition, a previously unheard-of wrestler won the tournament to the great surprise of all competitors. At the end of the tournament, to the great embarrassment of all the male competitors involved, the wrestler revealed herself to be a woman. Since then wrestlers have worn open-fronted jackets to be certain that this could not happen again!

Mongolians are obsessed with wrestling so there are stadia in most towns. Matches sometimes last a long time but may be over in seconds since they finish when any part of the loser's body, other than their feet, touches the ground. The ambition of professional wrestlers is to compete in the annual Nadaam festival, in which competitors represent their town and can rise through the ranks. The highest rank is Invincible-Titan and any wrestler reaching these lofty heights will become a national celebrity. The most famous wrestler is named Bat-Erdene, who carried the country's flag in the Sydney Olympics and incredibly won 42% of the national vote as the presidential candidate of the Mongolian Peoples' Party in the 2013 general election. He now owns a university that trains wrestlers, coaches and other sportsmen. The passion that Mongolians have for wrestling was illustrated in the 2016 Rio Olympics, when after their competitor controversially lost the bronze medal match, his two coaches stripped off to their pants and squared up to the judges, aggressively performing the *devee* dance!

Leaving the city, we ascended a tarmac road over a small pass with large grassy meadows full of gers to the north and the south. An irrigation channel had been built and part of the bank was supported by an old car that was completely buried in mud! Many passing cars honked at us as we climbed up the pass and shouts of encouragement followed us as we progressed. After cycling over the top then down the other side, we left the main road to take a short-cut through a river rather than making a five-kilometre detour over the bridge further to the south. Many vehicles had done the same thing, carving out a track that we followed down to the riverbank. Phil stopped to reattach his panniers which had become unclipped from the rack, while I looked for a suitable place to cross the river. I found a spot that was knee-deep, so we waded through and joined the road on the other side. The road was no longer tarmac, having become a dirt track once more heading north towards Uvs Nuur.

The track had a good surface to start with, hard-packed and stony, so we made timely progress away from the mountains. The vegetation surrounding Ulaangom began thinning out, the ecosystem becoming a much drier and sandier desert once more. Sparse shrubs still grew but there was clearly infrequent rainfall in this area in comparison to the fertile grasslands. Lizards scampered across the track in front of us and large camouflaged insects including giant grasshoppers hid in the grass. A few tiny jumping rodents called jerboa, ran away from us as we approached, and eagles circled overhead looking for prey. As we passed the last of the buildings and gers, which had been sporadically built close to the road near Ulaangom, our track turned east and became bumpier and sandier. This made pedalling more difficult due to the increased drag. To give ourselves a more comfortable ride and to allow our bikes to float better over the soft sandy surface, we let a little air pressure out of our tyres to make them softer and create a higher surface area in contact with the ground. Looking to the north, Uvs Nuur dominated the horizon. It was now clear enough for us to see beyond the lake where a large Russian mountain range was visible. Apparently, it is not uncommon for Russians to cross the border to steal horses from the Mongolian nomads living in the desert. As a result, there is great mistrust of Russians amongst the locals in the area surrounding Uvs Nuur.

Our road often split, so it took careful map reading to make sure we stayed on the correct track. The free open-source maps on our phones were good enough to include all of the small jeep tracks, so we could easily check that we were heading in the right direction. For the first 20 kilometres the track was not too difficult to ride on and would have been easily passable, if slightly more slowly, on a normal bike.

After the first section however, the surface consisted of rutted sand and would not have been rideable without the extra surface area provided by our four-inch-wide tyres, reducing the pressure we exerted on the road. Our fatbikes had been awesome so far but we were blown away by their performance in the desert. They really are the ultimate choice for off-road touring. This was one of the sections that the German couple we had met on the first evening in Mongolia had been forced to walk across, at what would have been about a quarter of our cycling speed.

Looking ahead to the east was much the same as looking behind to the west. There was very little to see, no features and no sign that we were making any progress across the seemingly endless landscape. To the north the unchanging Uvs Nuur horizon didn't help, but to the south, the Khan Khokhii Mountains did provide a changing feature proving that we were indeed moving forwards and helping us to fight the mental battle to continue. Long days in the desert can be mind-numbingly boring but I have found that if I can get into the right mindset, zoning out of the cycling, I am able to appreciate the incredible environment and make the most of the peaceful pressure-free time that I almost never have during day-to-day life. In hindsight, desert cycling is always fantastic, although at the time it is a struggle. On top of the mental battles, another challenge was the high temperature combined with a lack of shade. Since it was 33 degrees Celsius, in order to stay cool, it was important to regularly drink and not to overly exert ourselves. Fortunately, a slight tailwind was helping our progress and after a few hours we had covered 40 kilometres, at which point we stopped for lunch. Unfortunately, a bag of raisins, which we had purchased at the market in Ulaangom, also contained a few small stones, one of which I mistakenly tried to eat. It took a large chunk out of one of my wisdom teeth. It really hurt and I was worried about it becoming infected for the following few days because my gum swelled up painfully. Fortunately, it settled down after a while, perhaps with the help of some antibiotics that I had brought from home.

Unexpectedly, 67 kilometres from Ulaangom we came across a small truckers' stop, which sold drinks and very basic food, most of which had gone out of date. We stopped and sat in the shade drinking a sugary multivitamin drink and showing our route to the family that lived in the ger next-door. They were intrigued by the fatbikes and all had a go. They showed us their water pump that drew water up from a hole they had drilled in the ground, before offering us a shower. Drenching our heads under the cooling stream of water was wonderfully refreshing, before we waved goodbye and continued. The afternoon passed by in featureless desert miles as Uvs Nuur slowly came to an end. A few camel skulls lay near the roadside and every hour or so, a vehicle passed.

The highlight of the afternoon was provided by the herds of horses standing close to the roadside and sometimes watering themselves in puddles that had formed on the sandy track during the last rainfall. At one puddle the horses were rolling around in the wet mud to keep cool. They really are extraordinary creatures to be able to survive in such a harsh environment, with so little food and water. In addition, there is at least a 60 degrees Celsius temperature swing every year between summer and winter. We continued along the uneventful desert track until we had cycled 93 kilometres, at which point we pulled off the road to set up camp. Incredibly, as had often happened in Mongolia, 15 minutes later a nomad on a motorbike pulled up to say hello. He waved a pair of binoculars, which must have been how he had seen us so quickly from far away. I wondered if he was keeping an eye for Russian horse thieves. We cooked dinner and a pan full of tea before settling down for the night. The stars in the desert that night were breath-taking. They appeared so bright due to the lack of light pollution. I could see the glowing white band of the Milky Way stretching across the sky.

Wrestling statue in Ulaangom

A drier and sandier landscape in the Gobi Desert

Pleased to have fat tyres in the sand!

Unexpected respite in the desert

How do they survive out here?

Where to camp?

Day 6: Across more steppe
Distance travelled: 90.81 km

A man with acquaintances is the size of the steppe
- Mongolian proverb

I awoke to a strange noise at sunrise, comparable to a very loud creaking door. A beautiful view was visible through the opening of my tent door. Looking past the handlebars of my fatbike that lay outside, the sun was rising over the mountains to the south in front of a the perfectly peaceful desert. Exiting my tent to investigate the noise, I found its source to be an extensive line of camels striding across the sand. Three camels seem to be leading the group and were at least a kilometre ahead of those at the back. Baby camels walked alongside their mothers and the line seemed to be communicating by making the eerie, piercing, creaking noise. Phil emerged soon after me for a distinctly average breakfast of dried noodles and green tea. As we ate, the lead camels seemed to decide that they were heading in the wrong direction. For whatever reason they turned around, then the rest of the line followed moving back in the same direction from which they had come. Despite their slow lumbering motion, they moved surprisingly quickly across the sand, perfectly adapted to their environment. These Bactrian Camels have two humps and are considerably rarer than the single-humped variety. Most in Mongolia are domesticated so we assumed that these were probably owned by somebody, although the owner was nowhere to be seen. Bactrian Camels are incredibly tolerant of cold, heat, drought and high altitude, so became the animal of choice for the long-distance trade caravans of the Silk Road for many centuries. In Mongolia, they have been used by nomadic people for many years to carry heavy loads, particularly dismantled gers and possessions when searching for new pastures.

After packing up camp we were back on the track, now moving away from Uvs Nuur. A tailwind aided our progress once more as the sandy surface became stonier and more hard-packed, enabling us to ride at a higher speed. A few kilometres down the road we passed what looked like a large pump next to an industrial building that was standing on its own in the vast desert surroundings. We weren't sure what it was used for, speculating perhaps for pumping water or oil. A single worker passed us on a motorbike, looking rather hungover but waving friendlily at us nonetheless. As we approached the next town on our route, Zum Gobi, the desert seemed to be easing and the steppe started to become greener and less dry. Having climbed on a very slight gradient for the last 40 kilometres or so, it was a welcome relief when the road began descending into a river valley. The river ran through the desert, flowing from the mountains in the south to Uvs Nuur to the north. On either side of the river lush green grass grew, alongside bushes and a few trees. It was a long thin line of life in the otherwise barren steppe. Animals were drinking on the river bank, which seemed to be home to a variety of birds. Large cranes stood in the water on their long legs and a giant black pelican with a large bill descended, landing on the water like a large aircraft. Of course, the ever-present eagles were in attendance and what looked like a species of duck was paddling across the surface. We took the opportunity to have a wash and to clean our cycling clothes. Since it was so hot we were able to wash the clothes that we were wearing, put them on again and within 30 minutes or so, they would be completely dry. Having been coated in desert dust for the past 24 hours it was a great feeling to be clean again.

A soft sandy track climbed away from the river before ascending a small pass. In front of us was the small but welcoming settlement of Zum Gobi, above which circled even more large birds-of-prey. Despite seeing hundreds of eagles and other hawks in Mongolia I was still transfixed by the perfection of their evolution, with their muscular wings, long talons, curved pointy beaks and beady, far-seeing eyes. In Zum Gobi we found a great little café run by a lady and her daughter. Entering, we sat by the counter and ordered two slices of homemade pizza each along with unlimited milky tsai and five large, freshly made buuz. Surprisingly for such a small town, there was also a large grocery store, which had a lot of produce from Edeka, a German supermarket chain. This was a welcome surprise since we had been expecting more super noodles and out of date choco pies. Instead we bought chocolate-covered raisins, ice creams, pasta with tomato sauce and lots more sugary goodies. Strangely, despite the relatively simple building and basic looking town, the small shop had six CCTV cameras along with a computer screen, monitoring every corner of the room. After loading up the bikes we left the town under an overcast sky. The weather was changing as the sunny morning gave way to dark clouds, from which fell localised and very heavy rain.

Another sandy track led us out of the town and into green and barren steppe, with no gers, animals or buildings in sight. We struggled against a headwind for 20 kilometres or so, during which time the horizon didn't change at all. A few locals came over to say hello, including a couple of motorbike-riding nomads wearing their traditional outfit. We hadn't seen it worn much up to that point and it felt as though we were now entering a more traditionally Mongolian area, as opposed to the far west, which is majority Kazakh. The two male motorcyclists wore the *deel*, which is a three-quarter length gown that buttons up at the right shoulder to a high round-necked collar. One of the men wore a maroon-coloured deel, the other a grey-blue. Traditionally, Mongols wear a thick sheepskin deel lined with cotton in the winter and a thinner, patterned silk one in the summer. The motorcyclists also wore a long cloth belt wound several times around their waists. Both men and women wear this outfit, but strangely a man's belt is either three or five metres long (an odd number) and a woman's either two or four metres long (an even number). These two Mongols broke from custom as they were wearing trainers and caps, not the knee-length leather boots (gutal) and fur or leather hats that more traditional nomads would wear.

Our next visitor approached at the point where the barren desert steppe ended and an area of much more fertile grassland began. Thousands of animals were grazing and hundreds of gers were dotted in every direction. He approached, expertly galloping on a large brown horse. Nearing us, he began to dismount before the horse was stationary and hopped down next to us, a large smile on his young healthy-looking face. He looked at our bikes as we waved at him but didn't approach. Then he remounted and galloped off to his sheep and goat herd nearby. Children grow up quickly in Mongolia and it appeared that this teenager was responsible, at least in part, for a few hundred animals, which would likely make up the majority of his family's wealth. These children may not be as academically able as those in the western world but were already able to survive and flourish in this harsh environment, and able to look after themselves far better than children in the west. For the Mongolian nomad, skills such as the ability to ride a horse, build a ger and look after a herd are much more important than an academic education.

As the number of animals and nomads decreased once more, so did the quality of the grass. We were again cycling through the barren steppe. Phil got another puncture, although it was slow enough that we could pump it up regularly to keep it topped up with air and continue to the campsite that night. We planned to reach a river that was marked on the map, hoping to be able to wash before bed. The next 15 kilometres or so dragged by without incident and eventually we reached our intended destination. Unfortunately, the river had completely dried up but nevertheless, it was a wonderful place to camp. As we looked for a good spot to pitch the tents, we approached a guy kneeling on the side of the road. He noticed us when we were around ten metres away and jumped a mile, which we thought was very suspicious behaviour. He seemed to be hiding something, which looked like it may be the body of a large bird of prey. Was he hunting illegally? Continuing, we found a beautiful, flat, grassy campsite on the other side of the valley.

Fatbiking across Mongolia

We would be reaching another town very early the next day, so we used up most of our water for a few rounds of green tea while Phil fixed his puncture. As the sun set, I walked over to the only tree that grew for miles around. It was dying but on it was built a giant eagles' nest. Two large eagles sat in the tree, a perfect vantage point over the plain. The sunset behind the silhouetted tree was spectacular as the sky turned from blue, to yellow, to orange and finally to red. Back at the tent we used the incredible Google Skymaps app to identify the stars and planets that were appearing in the darkening night sky. We saw Jupiter, Saturn and Mars before the stars became visible, so much brighter than back home. Looking up at the Milky Way made me feel part of a much bigger world. Back home, where light pollution masks the sky, it is very easy to forget that we are part of a gigantic universe. In Mongolia, everything feels much bigger. Snapping me out of this feeling of tiny insignificance, I heard a male voice shouting at top of the dry river bank. We both waved at him as he came over asking for a drink. He downed a bottle of water then ate a few of our waffle biscuits. He explained that his motorbike had broken down about 30 kilometres away and that he had walked through the steppe with no food or water heading to the nearby town of Baruunturuum. We told him he had only eight kilometres left to walk and wished him luck. A couple of hours later, while in bed, I heard a truck passing by. Possibly he had found a friend to help him to pick up his motorbike. Mongolians travel very light given how far from civilisation their roads take them; a bottle of water and some food would have been very useful!

Looking out of my tent during sunrise

Bactrian Camels in the Gobi Desert

Valuable water for the wild horses

Eagles in Zum Gobi

A localised rainstorm over Zum Gobi

A teenage shepherd

Another lovely campsite

The only tree for miles around

Day 7: A plague of locusts and a storm
Distance travelled: 85.41 km

Thunderbolt and lightning, very very frightening
- Queen

With very little food left, we made do with just a few stale biscuits and a cup of tea to get us going that morning. Fortunately, just a few kilometres separated our campsite from the town of Baruunturuum. After around an hour of steady cycling we reached its outskirts, where a shallow river flowed under a wooden bridge. A quick wash in the crystal-clear water helped us to look slightly more respectable for breakfast in a café. It was still before nine o'clock when we found one, so it was only just opening. The chefs couldn't offer us any food from their menu as they were waiting for a delivery, so Phil went to the kitchen and pointed at some bread and eggs. It seems that they got the message. Twenty minutes later a giant deep-fried egg, tomato and spam sandwich was put in front of each of us. It was tasty but incredibly filling and very oily, so we felt rather lethargic after eating. A well-stocked shop and a petrol station allowed us to restock before heading out into the steppe once more. The riding that morning was uneventful and featureless for the next 20 kilometres or so, until we reached the small hamlet of Duruunturuum where we stopped in the shade of a derelict building full of noisy goats.

As we snacked on a Snickers each, a young boy approached nervously, riding his bike. I offered him a waffle biscuit, which seemed to provide him with confidence that we were alright, so he sat down next to us, staring at our fatbikes. Soon his father followed and showed us that his son's bike had a problem. One of the pedals was broken. The man, named Dorjdavaa, brought over a toolkit from his nearby ger, which we used to take off the pedal and inspect it. Unfortunately, it was damaged beyond repair and needed replacing so we were unable to help. Soon afterwards, Dorjdavaa invited us into his ger where we met his wife, Chimedregzen, as well as his daughter. Since it was hot and muggy outside and we both felt sleepy after our ridiculously large breakfast, we were very happy to spend an hour or so relaxing inside. Using a dictionary in the back of our guidebook we were able to communicate with the family. We drank tea and picked at bread, hazelnut chocolate spread and curd out of politeness as we were both still very full. Dorjdavaa told us that his family owned 30 sheep, 30 goats, a cow and a couple of horses. The lovely interior included a small dresser with lots of photos on display and a collection of medals that the son had won playing chess. It sounded like he was a very intelligent young boy and his father had great

53

aspirations for his future. Dorjdavaa had very bad burns on one of his arms. I think he said that he had hurt it when a pan of boiling water fell off the stove in the centre of the ger. Although they lived a fairly traditional lifestyle, the family were not nomadic and lived in this small village all year round. They seemed to have a very comfortable life.

Inside the ger were five beds, two cupboards, a solar powered television, various ornaments, decorative wall hangings, a cupboard full of tools and motorbike parts, a small kitchen area with various parts of sheep hanging behind a sheet and strips of curd hanging from the centre of the ger's ceiling to dry. Next to the stove in the middle of the ger was a large bucket of milk that was fresh from their cow that morning. The walls were made from patterned felt that was supported by a wooden trellis, coloured green with large red printed flowers. A small Buddhist shrine was set up on the northern wall of the ger, with a small statute of The Buddha as the central piece. As is typical for Mongolian gers, the door was positioned facing south to allow sunlight into the home and to face away from the cold northerly winds. Outside was a long-drop toilet inside a small shed that was next to a wooden frame for tying up horses. While we had been sitting inside it had rained quite heavily, but as soon as it stopped we all went outside and the boy and Dorjdavaa had a go on the fatbikes. As we departed we gave the family crayons for the children, fishing hooks and a candle. They gave us a large piece of curd each for the road.

Soon after we had left the friendly family, the rain started again and fell very heavily for an hour or so. Thunder shook the ground and lightning flashed on the horizon as the road became muddy and slippery. Fortunately, the storm soon passed and the sun returned to dry us out. The road was now passing through a beautiful grassy pasture with wildflowers growing everywhere we looked, including bright white edelweiss, large spherical blue thistles, dark purple orchids, as well as small yellow and large red flowers that I've not been able to identify. The ground was swarming with large grasshoppers and other insects. As we moved forwards the grasshoppers leapt upwards towards us. I concentrated hard, attempting not to crush the ones that jumped under my wheels. Many hovered by the path, their red wings flapping and making a loud buzzing noise. The road was bumpy, sandy and slow-going, but as always our fatbikes made the riding relatively easy. We cycled up and down small rolling hills, through a varied landscape with a constantly changing horizon and a fun descent around every corner. Eventually, the wild flower meadows gave way the first planted crops we had seen in Mongolia. Wheat was being grown in a vast field stretching as far as the eye could see. I imagined harvest time, when the local people would surely have their work cut out to collect their crop before winter arrived. To the north were a range of giant sand dunes in front of dark mountains on the Russian side of the border.

Stopping for a snack, we rested the bikes on the ground and sat on the roadside. After a few minutes, my bike was absolutely covered in small sweat bees. Phil thought that they were stingless but it was nerve-racking to pick up my bike and cycle off with probably a hundred-or-so bees swarming around me. Since it was early evening, we needed to quickly pass through the field of wheat to find a spot to pitch the tents before sunset. We cycled later than normal that evening, until we had rounded the northern end of a long mountain range. Now very close to the Russian border and cycling on a relatively high area of land, we looked out over a beautiful mountainous landscape that was coated in places with the first large pine forests we had seen in Mongolia. Finally, we exited the wheat fields and re-entered the beautiful wildflower meadows. A Toyota Prius hybrid pulled up with two guys driving to Ulaanbaatar. I couldn't believe they were driving such an unsuitable car along this sandy jeep track. I used to have one as a company car and found it to be excellent on long road journeys but equally learned that it was distinctly average off-road. They told us that it would take them at least two days to reach their destination before kindly passing us two bottles of water and wishing us luck.

At the first opportunity, we pulled onto the land just off the side of the road and pitched the tents. Our wild camping spot had a very remote feel to it with nothing man-made in sight. To the south were large mountains, which concerned me slightly as I had read that wolves lived there, and we were very far from civilisation. After we went to bed the rain started once more and soon became a thunderstorm. The weather turned fierce, with intense winds and horizontal heavy rain. My one-man tent was waterproof but, unfortunately, Phil's wasn't so slowly leaked for around four hours during which the storm raged. I was counting the seconds between the thunder and lightning, from which you can calculate how far away the storm is. At one point the thunder came almost directly after the lightning, which was terrifying as the whole sky flashed and the ground shook. I was worried that we would be struck but we escaped unscathed. I only slept for about three hours that night.

A typical Mongolian shop

Dorjdavaa and family

Grass-covered hills

Cranes in the grasslands

Day 8: Into the heartland

Distance travelled: 81.79 kilometres

Mongolian herders have a reverence for the land although many will tell you they don't know why that feel that way.
- Anonymous

It was an eventful start to the day. As we cooked breakfast, the short pipe linking Phil's petrol stove to the fuel bottle split and a jet of petrol squirted onto the flames. The petrol exploded in a pretty spectacular fireball and thereafter the stove was unusable. Fortunately, neither of us was hurt, nor were our tents or clothes damaged. Since the coffee that we had been heating up was already fairly warm and the only casualty was the stove, we considered ourselves rather fortunate. Very tired, I needed the caffeine that morning to help to wake me up. My storm-interrupted sleep had been further disturbed by dreams of wolves coming down from the nearby mountains to attack us. Fortunately, there was no sign of the wolves or the storm and the track was already drying out in the early morning sunlight.

Rounding the edge of the long mountain range, we started heading southeast, away from the Russian border. The long wildflower-filled grasslands were behind us and we were now cycling through plains covered in short, green, spiky grass. A large Toyota Landcruiser towing a giant oil container passed us, but that was the only vehicle we saw on the road all morning. Large, rocky, ominous-looking mountain ranges ran in parallel lines either side of the road that was leading us to a small pass on the far side of the grassy plain. Localised rain passed overhead, showering us with refreshing and cooling drops of water for a few minutes every hour or so. The climb up the pass was short and as we reached the top, a stunning view greeted us. A long descent to a wide river floodplain lay ahead, which would return us to the seemingly endless grasslands inhabited by many more nomadic families. We had made it across the barren desert and steppe, which separates the sparsely populated Kazakh dominated west of the country from the central area, populated by descendants of the Mongol Khans themselves. A staggering fact is that around eight percent of men living in the area covered by the former gigantic Mongol empire, are descended from Genghis Khan. This translates to half a percent of the world's population, which is quite a genetic legacy!

As we reached the floodplain, the comparatively large town of Tes was visible ahead. The first sizeable pine forest, which the track passed in close proximity to, grew near the river and provides a building material that those living in the west of the country do not have access to. The houses in Tes were mainly Swiss-style pine cabins surrounded by the picturesque hills on the far side of the floodplain, which was dotted with idyllically situated gers. Having been in such barren scenery for so long, the sharp contrast to this gorgeous scene was wonderful. We both snapped thirty-or-so photos before crossing the plain and reaching Tes. In one of the log cabins was a basic café selling buuz as usual, which we always looked forward to eating, despite the rather bland taste.

Tes also contained a good size grocery store outside of which was a large crowd of people. It seemed that a bus had just arrived from Ulaanbaatar, containing family members from other areas of the country who had come to visit Tes. Some of the town's inhabitants were already celebrating with bottles of vodka and were very keen that the two western cyclists should join them. We approached warily, smelling the familiar stench of stale vodka on the men's breath, but soon relaxed as we were offered the customary snuff bottle, which I accepted, taking a sniff and nodding approvingly without really knowing what I was supposed to be smelling. One of the visitors from Ulaanbaatar was a well-dressed young lady who was an English teacher. She spoke perfect English and told us that she was visiting her parents for a few weeks during the summer holidays. She was very interested in where we were going but, as was the case with many people we spoke to in Mongolia, not at all surprised that we were cycling across the country, nor that we were cycling rather a long way. Long journeys are a normal part of Mongolian culture and although we were not using the traditional form of transport, what we were doing did not seem as unusual to the local people as it does in most other countries. Her father approached with a snuff bottle but no vodka smell. He was not wearing the traditional deel robe, but a striped suit jacket, a green shirt and a dark grey trilby hat. We were told he was 87, which is extremely old for a Mongolian. Either side of him were drunk men wearing the traditional nomadic outfit. An unusually tall Mongolian stood to his left, wearing a light green deel, along with a bright orange silk belt and an army-camouflage patterned brimmed hat. On the other side was a man wearing a pattered brown deel and a red baseball cap. It seemed that most Mongolian men wore hats but not necessarily of a traditional style. These men were not nomads but still had strong nomadic routes. Typically, nomadic men are not heavy drinkers since they do not generally have a lot of money and spend so much time on horseback, minding their animals. Those who have settled however, seem to have fallen into the trap of many former

Soviet-influenced countries where vodka flows freely, and alcohol related problems are widespread.

After posing for lots of photos, we locked up the bikes and purchased supplies. We didn't need much since the next town was only a few hours' ride over the mountains that lay ahead of us to the east. A refreshing ice cream was most welcome in the heat of the sun. We refilled our fuel bottle with petrol for the stove that we hoped we would be able to fix. Waving goodbye to our new acquaintances we set off in the direction of the next town, named *Bayentes*. Looking back on the trip, this road was one of the highlights of our adventure. It is one of the best sections of cycle touring I have ever experienced, climbing over three passes in the lush green mountains between the two towns. Rocky peaks in spectacular shapes looked as though they would provide world-class climbing routes, but better than them were the cycling trails. Motorbikes had carved their own paths through the mountains to avoid the rutted jeep tracks. These thin tracks were wide enough for a motorbike tyre but no wider. At corners, dirt had become piled up on the outside of the bend forming a bank that provided a camber, allowing us to carry our speed. The trails curved around obstacles and followed the contours of the land. They were at least as good as any manufactured bike trail and incredibly fun to ride. Adding to that, the wonderful and unique scenery of Mongolia, the wild horses, the serene silence of the steppe, the rocky peaks, the river to the north, the pine forests, the mountain slopes and the endless blue sky, it made for an incredible afternoon of cycling.

The steepest uphill sections of the road to Bayentes tested our gears, and Phil did very well with a more limited range than those on my bike, to clear all sections of the trail. Not far out of Tes, we turned down another kind offer from two motorcyclists to share their bottle of vodka. After passing over the third mountain pass we reached the final and best descent, which ended on the edge of Bayentes. The track skirted the bottom of a rocky peak, then following singletrack to another town made from log cabins. Although it had not been our plan to stay there that night, the large sign above a room with the word "*hotel*" in large letters persuaded us to change our mind. It soon became clear that the description of the establishment on the sign was far from accurate and that what was on offer was actually a room with a couple of beds in it. There was a toilet around the back of the building in a hut, a garage for the bikes and after enquiring about washing, we were told that the price included a lift to the river that was a 20-minute drive away... perfect!

A quick trip to the restaurant next-door refuelled us with a large tasty bowl of mutton and noodle soup, before two young guys, named Batbayar and Bolormaa, met us and drove us to the river in a small minibus. I was most impressed with their self-imposed rules about washing clothes. Presumably because detergent pollutes the water in the river, they asked to wash our clothes a couple of metres away from the bank using a plastic bowl. The River Tes was wide and unspoilt, with fast flowing clear water, and these two young men wanted to keep it that way. Their desire to protect their environment was admirable and an attitude that much of the rest of the world could learn from. The respect that Mongolians have for nature also comes from the days of the great Khans who introduced laws to protect the environment. Genghis Khan forbade his soldiers from bathing in rivers or streams and the punishment for damaging the steppe with excavation or fire was death. Fortunately for us bathing in rivers is no longer prohibited, so we had a refreshing wash then a swim in the fast-flowing water.

An alarmingly high-speed 20-minute drive later and we were back at the room where we drank a couple of beers, caught up on diary entries, looked over our maps and charged our devices, before going to bed. At that point there was a knock on the door so we both got up again. Our two new friends had returned and were very eager to find out more about our travels. An hour and a half of pointing at maps and scrolling though photos on my camera followed. We were tired and wanted to get a good night's sleep, but it was rewarding to be able to share our experiences with the friendly young Mongolians. They were fascinated to see so much of their country through our photos. They wanted to hear about England and I supposed that much of our equipment was fascinating to them, since it was not available to purchase within their country. It is likely that we were the first British people they had ever met, so it was important to be friendly and respectful of their culture, in order that they got a good impression of ours. Eventually their mother appeared and asked them to leave us, at which point we both collapsed into our beds exhausted after another action-packed day.

Mongolia's beauty from our campsite

Approaching Tes

Friendly locals in the centre of Tes

Possibly the best cycling of the trip on the road between Tes and Bayantes

The reason why we came to Mongolia

Is there anywhere more beautiful on Earth?

Entering Bayantes

The River Tes, where we were taken to wash

Day 9: Nomad hospitality
Distance travelled: 79.43 km

The ger is a rich and happy abode,
On firm birch props,
Clustered with animals
- Extract from a song by an unknown writer

We started the ninth day of our Mongolian adventure very tired after our late-night chat with Batbayar and Bolormaa. There was a small wooden table in the centre of our room, at which we had a leisurely breakfast of bread and Nutella as well as a mug of coffee that had been brought to us by the friendly lady who owned the room. Leaving the small town, we began climbing up a wide plain that had an almost constant gradient for about 20 kilometres. It was as though the whole landscape had been tilted by about five degrees, which made for a demoralising ascent since it looked flat and our progress towards the horizon felt snail-paced. This, along with the headwind and the gloomy overcast weather, made for a difficult morning, further complicated by the vicious dogs that lived at each ger. We fended off the dogs by stopping and throwing rocks in their direction whenever they sprinted towards us, barking. Fortunately we survived these terrifying experiences unscathed. Our moods improved when the wind changed near the top of the pass, becoming a tailwind and assisting us over the 1,700-metre summit. Behind us was a gigantic cumulonimbus cloud, more epic than any I have ever seen because it dominated the horizon of the gigantic Mongolian landscape. Every few minutes the sky flashed and a fork of lightning fired out of the bottom of the cloud... it was catching up with us. Fortunately, a strong tailwind and a long downhill led us away from the path of the storm, which just missed us passing by to the south.

When we reached the bottom of the descent the track rounded a mountain that hosted many herds of grazing sheep and goats. Soon a spectacular view of the River Tes materialised in front of us. A much wider floodplain than that on the previous day was covered with gers in every direction and our road led us close to many of them, which was both a blessing and a curse. The constant threat of dogs kept us alert but the kindness of the local people meant that we were very keen to approach their homes. Our first interaction with the nomads in that area was initiated by about ten young children who spotted us from a long way away. As we approached their homes, they sprinted out to meet us on the nearby track. We

66

stopped as they approached, waving and smiling. As they got closer they became wary of us and stopped, until their fathers caught up on horseback, closely followed by their mothers. About twenty people now surrounded us and started pointing, chatting and laughing. Soon they were admiring the fatbikes and then having a go on each of them. They then offered us a go on the horses. Getting up onto the saddles was unnerving! I felt very high up and unstable as the horse moved around beneath me. Clearly riding a horse is a very effective way of getting around in Mongolia but having tried both, my preference is definitely a fatbike!

We waved goodbye to the friendly locals as we struggled along a muddy road section, which confirmed that it had been a great idea to pay for accommodation the previous night since it had rained for most of it. Reaching the river bank, we stopped for lunch at one of an infinite number of perfect picnic spots. Close to us were a few gers built next to the Tes Gol, which we were still following. The nearest ger was about one hundred metres away from where we sat. Close to the ger and directly on the river bank was a bright orange modern tent. We had not seen an object of this colour since arriving in Mongolia and the tent looked incredibly out of place in this traditional unspoilt landscape. We thought perhaps, that western tourists may have asked to camp near to the ger.

As we were eating lunch a young couple came out of the tent, before they spotted us and waved. Then two teenage girls came out of the ger approaching us slowly, closely followed by their father. They were a reserved family, which is unusual for Mongolians. As they got close we waved and beckoned them over, sharing some of our sweets with them. We offered them a go on the bikes and one of the girls tried riding mine but struggled with the weight so didn't get far. Soon afterwards, the couple came over and it became clear that they were Mongolian too, but from a very different world. The young man, wearing western clothing, was tall and stocky with a smart haircut and a kind, friendly face. He walked hand-in-hand with his pretty girlfriend who was short, had long straight black hair, wore jeans, converse shoes and a bright orange t-shirt, which matched the tent. The young man asked "*Sprichst du Deutsch*?" to which Phil replied "*ja*" and I replied "*ein bisschen*". Phil lived in Germany for several years and studied the language at university so is fluent, and I can get by, having lived in Munich for six months. The young man, named Noyon, was fluent too and was studying German at the university in Ulaanbaatar. He explained that he and his girlfriend lived in Ulaanbaatar and were visiting his family together for the first time. They were loving their time in the beautiful countryside away from the bustling metropolis and were planning a two-week tour of the country before returning. We asked him about our route and he explained that there were no shops in the next small village but that we would reach a town with shops and a café the next day. Meanwhile, the father had discovered that western men have hairy legs, which he found most amusing. He pulled on my leg hair, which was quite painful... perhaps he was not so reserved after all! Finishing our lunch, we packed up our bags once more before waving farewell to the latest friendly family.

Continuing up along the dirt-track on the river bank, which was drying out in the midday sun, we entered a pine forest. Mosquitoes buzzed around our heads once more in the muggy air. We passed over long sections of slippery muddy road, which dramatically slowed our progress, although the track was just rideable due to the traction provided by our fatbike tyres. As the road led away from the river it gained height, leaving the cover of the pine trees that grew on the bank. The riding became easier since there was no standing water on the steeper section of the road. As we cruised along a downhill section, I spotted a smaller trail heading southeast, which looked to cut off a corner of the main trail, a possible shortcut? We decided to try it out, keen to leave the main track and explore the side valley, which had been formed by a tributary of the Tes River that our route now took us along. Following the bumpy track, we saw a couple of teenage boys riding bareback horses and who seemed entirely unsurprised to see us. They nodded as we passed them, both continuing on our respective ways. Soon the track petered out and became a wide grassy plain that was still a great surface to ride on. There was no issue with navigation since we just needed to head up the valley and therefore couldn't go wrong. The river in the middle of the valley was narrow and looked simple to cross so we pointed our bikes in the right direction and rode south towards a cluster of around 20 gers spread over an area of around a square kilometre forming a Mongolian hamlet. Unusually some of the gers were blue and were the first non-white gers that we had seen.

Approaching the gers, we were soon spotted by one of the families. A large group of smiling faces beckoned us over. A pair of identical twins around the age of 12 looked like a real handful for their caring, calm mother. Wearing identical outfits of bright blue tracksuit bottoms, long leather riding boots and stripy sweatshirts, they ran around with endless energy and straight away asked for a go on the bikes. The twins were small and very confident but I was concerned about handing our bikes over to them, since they were so heavy compared to the boys. As soon as they began riding though it was clear that my concerns were unnecessary. Both had incredibly good balance, which was more impressive since they were unable to sit down properly as the saddles were too high. They whizzed around in circles until they finally ran out of energy and returned to the ger. Their elder brother then wanted a go. He looked about 15, was very tall, full of energy and seemingly very excited to have met us. He kept one of his eyes shut most of the time, probably to help correct the squint that he had. In the UK, he would have had this sorted out as a baby, illustrating the relative poverty of the Mongolian nomadic lifestyle. He wore a long green deel tied with a golden yellow belt, leather riding boots and a New York Yankees cap.

After riding the bike, the teenager insisted that we had a go on his horse that he expertly rode over from an area where all the family horses were tied to large vertical posts, close to the gers. As he approached, he stopped the horse, made it lift its front eft leg up, then moved sideways before galloping round in a circle. Phil and I didn't display the same prowess when sitting on the horse as we were led around in a circle. Phil though, did seem a lot more confident than I felt when I sat on the saddle, feeling a very long way from the ground. Once back on solid ground we met the rest of the family, beginning with a formal introduction to the eldest member. It seemed that this family were wealthy enough to have a ger that was solely used for social purposes, which allowed the beds to be situated in a separate one and provided more room in the ger where the family ate. We were ushered inside where the old man sat calmly and proudly, offering us a seat on the blanket-covered bench to the right of his armchair. The customary snuff bottle was offered, wh ch we sniffed, then nodded our approval before passing it back. This man was the grandfather of the twins and teenager and would have overseen the most important family decisions such as purchasing food, selling animals and where to set up the gers. It seemed that everyday life though was led by the twins' mother rather than their father, who seemed to be quite lazy, ate a lot and appeared to have rather a pleasant existence!

The mother was a very impressive lady and when she asked her children to do something, the order was followed instantly and precisely. She brough: over a gigantic snack including a large bowl of fried bread, homemade goats cheese and curd as well as a tub of homemade yak butter that was more like clotted cream. Mugs of milky tsai were passed around as we ate our fill of the delicious food. Having assumed that this very generous offering was to be the whole meal that we would be eating with the family, we were very full by the stage at which that they offered us a hot meal. Not wishing to be rude and curious to try more local food, we enthusiastically agreed despite not feeling at all hungry. We communicated with the lady of the house while she prepared the meal, through photos, drawing and miming It transpired that she was a local doctor serving the community of

69

gers in the surrounding area. They owned a jeep which she used to get around, as well as a solar powered phone system that was connected to a large mast and allowed people in neighbouring valleys to call for help. She was clearly the breadwinner and the source of the family's wealth. Since they had a solid and reliable income they did not have a herd, owning just ten cows, one yak and one goat. In addition to the jeep, they had two motorbikes and four horses.

After discussing these subjects with the family, we passed around photos from home along with my camera, which I used to show them the photos that we had taken on our journey through their country so far. The children's father was fascinated to see areas of his country that he had never been to. A large bowl of fresh sugared redcurrants was passed round, picked from the bushes that grew next to the nearby stream. Meanwhile, the children were taking it in turns to whack what looked like beef jerky with a large hammer. It turned out to be dried yak meat that was going to be put into the large pan in which our meal was being prepared. The pan sat on a cast iron stove in the centre of the ger and while the boys prepared the meat, their mother cut noodle dough into small pieces ending up with what looked like rectangular shaped pieces of gnocchi, which she threw into the pan in small batches. After leaving the broth to cook for a few minutes it was announced that it was ready, at which point everybody from the extended family entered the ger. There were at least ten people inside, sat cross-legged on the floor except for the eldest male, Phil and me. We attempted, but failed, to give up our seats, before being passed the two largest bowls of noodle and yak meat soup followed by the yak butter in its large tub. The twins motioned for us to scoop out a dollop of the butter and add it to the soup. The food was delicious; by far the best food we had experienced in rural Mongolia. I ate my first bowl and then before I knew what was happening, I was given a second. Completely stuffed, I managed to eat the soup while considering that it was unlikely that much cycling would happen that afternoon! As soon as it became clear that Phil and I had eaten all we could, the mother let the boys finish the pot. They descended on it like gannets, polishing off the rest of the soup in less than a minute. We were very impressed by their politeness, waiting for us to eat everything we wanted before finishing it off. If I had known that they were waiting for us to finish, I would not have had a second helping! I imagine that this is a Mongolian custom, since guests at yurts are often on long journeys and are likely to need large meals.

Soon after we had finished, the family asked if we wanted to spend the night with them. We politely declined since it was still early in the afternoon and we had a long way to go. The family had been unbelievably kind, sharing what they had with us to support our journey. We looked through our kit to see what we could give them as gifts, finding the following; two Snickers for the twins, a waterproof dry-bag for the teenager, a bandage for the mother, a t-shirt for the father, some batteries and a fishing hook. After one last tsai we said goodbye. An aunt and uncle were also leaving, dressed in their best traditional clothing for a trip to the town of Bayentes that we had cycled from that morning. Leaving the ger in the bright sunshine, we looked around the beautiful valley in which the family lived. The mother had told us that they weren't nomadic and lived on that patch of land all year round. It was an idyllic spot. I reflected that they had chosen the location of their permanent home well. As we cycled away, waving, the three children ran to their horses, jumped on their backs and raced after us. As a group of five, we rode together for a kilometre or so across the valley until we reached the main track again. The control that those boys had over their animals was very impressive as we sped across the plain, just metres from the galloping animals. What an exhilarating experience!

Eventually parting from the children Phil and I continued alone, humbled by the hospitality of the nomads. The kindness and spirit of this remote and sparsely populated community is something that the western world could learn a lot from. The track took us along a small stream, passing more gers in which sat families who would have all fed us and offered us a place to stay if needed. One is never far from help in Mongolia. Continuing around a small hillock, on which herds of goats and sheep grazed, we approached the wide floodplain of the River Tes once more. In the distance was a high mountain range in front of which lay a gigantic, flat, deep-green pasture. Trees and bushes grew near to the riverside, which was much narrower and flowed less quickly than it had done further down the valley in the towns of Bayentes and Tes. We left the track and approached a meander of the river, finding a perfect campsite on the flat, soft grass above the water. There was an endless supply of bone-dry firewood as well as a lovely still pool on the outside of the river bend, perfect for a wash. We finished our day slightly earlier than normal, set up camp, got ready for bed then made a fire, which we used to cook noodles and heat tea. Phil had not pegged his tent down, which was unfortunately caught by a gust of wind and blew into the river! I rolled around on the floor laughing as Phil jumped in after it. At this point I suppose I could have been more helpful but with the warm fire was hard to leave! Phil waded out of the river with his tent and pegged it down. It dried quickly in the evening sunlight. No harm done. This had been the best day so far, dominated by the kindness of strangers.

71

Homemade bread, cheese and yak butter

Phil horse riding

Life on the steppe

The kindest family we met

Yak meat and noodle soup

How could we not stop to camp here?

Campsite on the river bend

Boiling water in mess tins

Day 10: Goulash and buuz

Distance travelled: 86.25 km

Joyful is he at whose door guests' horses are always tethered
- Mongolian proverb

We awoke to the peaceful sound of flowing water. Enough wood remained from the previous night for us to relight the fire to cook pot noodles along with a mug of tea for breakfast. As we ate, a nomad on a horse herded a gigantic muscular bull across the river, waving at us but not batting an eyelid at the unusual inhabitants of the river bend. The rider galloped along one side of the bull to steer it in the opposite direction and used a long whip to keep it moving. It looked like a dangerous beast and was far larger than the man's horse. Eventually he persuaded it to cross the river to an area where a herd of cows were grazing. Perhaps this bull was shared by the local inhabitants for breeding with their herds.

Shortly afterwards another nomad on horseback directed a herd of cows along the river, past our tents and out into the pastures beyond the woods on the river bank. When passing he motioned behind and in front of him; the international sign language for where have you been, where are you going? We called after him, Bayantes, Khövsgöl Nuur, which was our next major destination. His saddle was made from beautiful waxed leather with patterns embroidered into it. He also held a long whip and wore a dark-blue deel with leather riding boots. Unfortunately, my beautiful leather saddle made by the world-famous British company, *Brooks*, had developed a problem with the tension bolt that keeps the leather tight. It had sagged in the middle and I didn't have the tools to fix it. I ended up using a spare ratchet strap to pull the front of the saddle down towards the top tube of my bike frame, adding tension to it. The saddle became much more comfortable and the bodge lasted for the duration of the trip.

We packed up quickly and set off along the river bank, following the herdsman who was travelling at a leisurely pace. Cranes floated on the river and flew overhead. In all directions, the sky was dotted with swooping hawks. There was no track along the side of the river but our fatbikes didn't struggle on the grassy earth that led us to the tiny settlement of *Haboom*, consisting of three farm buildings with red tin roofs. We were back on the *Northern Road*, which was now a dry dirt track that passed a ger every few minutes. Friendly as ever, the locals waved after us as we cycled past and children ran over to the road for high fives. A few dogs approached us but our tactic of getting off the bikes and staring them down worked well, so none got too close that day. A couple of small passes allowed us to take a direct route over the hills rather than following long meanders of the river. This also kept the riding interesting, since we were climbing and descending rather than plodding over flat ground. The now stony road was very bumpy, causing our arms to take a pounding as we descended towards the river once more. Having eaten most of our food supply we were left with only raisins, peanuts and sweets and were both very hungry. I was regretting giving our two remaining Snickers to the twins the previous afternoon! We were struggling with depleted energy reserves and were battling a headwind along the ever-present River Tes.

After almost a full morning's ride we finally reached the bridge that would take us over the river and into the town of Tsetserleg. As ever, the nomad population increased as we approached the town and huge numbers of animals were living on the grasslands. Two young herdsmen on small horses galloped in circles around a group of gigantic shaggy yaks, moving them across the road. Meanwhile we climbed up a small pass and were greeted at the top by a group of drunk Mongolians who were celebrating a birthday party, singing at the top of their voices and sharing chocolate liquors that they encouraged us to try. With delicious alcohol-filled chocolate in our mouths, we descended into the town for a much-needed break in a café. It was a beautiful little place made once again from log cabins, with immaculately-kept wide street-lit roads that contained plenty of places to eat. We picked the first; a shabbily-decorated room separated into booths that each contained a table and a few plastic chairs. It seemed like luxury at the time. Walking over to the kitchen I saw a giant cauldron of stew and a massive pan full of rice. Decision made, I ordered two generous portions, alongside a large salad, potatoes, and a large flask of milky tea. Minutes later it all arrived and cost only the equivalent of five pounds. The guy on the table next to us performed charades to act out the animal that we had just eaten. We had assumed that it had been mutton, but eventually we worked out that it was marmot. Using the dictionary in the back of our guidebook, we confirmed this by saying *"tarvag?"* to which he nodded enthusiastically. Hoping that we would not contract the bubonic plague, which is carried by marmots in Mongolia, we left the restaurant and headed to a supermarket. After stocking up on large quantities of food (we were not going to run low again) and an ice cream for dessert, we left the town via a hasty stop at a long-drop on the outskirts of town. We had just eaten a large quantity of food and had not eating properly that morning, so our digestive systems were both struggling!

A non-eventful, quiet afternoon followed as we passed over a series of beautiful grassy hills. We slowly gained altitude until we reached around 2,000 metres. The road ascended a series of slopes between flat plains, so we climbed then coasted along before climbing again. This was repeated several times as we made seemingly little progress into the vast horizon of grasslands that rose ahead of us. The lower green meadows of the valley gave way to an endless sea of longer grass dotted with wildflowers and inhabited by thousands of small grey marmots that provided a soundtrack to our progress in the form of their warning call. Looking a long way ahead and scanning the undergrowth, I could see the small creatures standing up on their hind legs and looking around. As we approached they sounded a warning call and darted head-first down a nearby hole, their bushy tails following close behind!

An hour or so after leaving Tsetserleg we came across a couple of guys who had been riding a motorbike. They waved us down and animatedly shook a punctured inner tube at us. I confirmed that it would be no problem to fix and as I did so, Phil took care of the usual *where have you come from, where are you going* conversation. A couple of minutes later, I handed back the mended inner tube along with a few biscuits before waving farewell. We were getting into the Mongolian spirit, *be helped by and help others*, which has sustained nomadic travellers for centuries. Incidentally, when telling others that we had come from Tsetserleg, it was rather confusing since there are a few towns with that name in close vicinity. Mongolia has an issue with both town names and street names as they don't seem to have a great deal of imagination when it comes to naming places. They have recently had to rename many streets across the country, since there were so many called "*Chingghis Khan Street*" (the Mongolian version of Genghis). Apparently, the limited postal service had been struggling to find anybody's address!

Not long after the motorbike puncture repair, a large Toyota four-wheel drive vehicle pulled up alongside us. A Dutch couple sat within and told us about their journey. They were on a year-long trip overland to Australia, having driven to Mongolia from the Netherlands. They seemed to be having some fun but all-in-all were downbeat about their recent experiences. They, like us, had fallen in love with the wonderful scenery in Mongolia, but in their large vehicle were quite removed from the country and its people. We told them about our experiences of sharing meals with nomads and swapping our bikes for horses, which they had not been able to do. Behind the doors of a giant vehicle, complete with satellite internet, an iPad and a windscreen, the endless grasslands seemed monotonous to them. The relative advantages of travelling by bike were more obvious to us than ever.

We had covered a good distance that afternoon so were ready to find a campsite. Finally reaching a highpoint in the vast landscape, we were looking down on what lay ahead rather than up at it. There were no trees at all, just endless rolling grasslands. A pleasant smell of wild herbs hung in the air as we approached a broken-down vehicle. The driver and passengers were awaiting rescue from a friend who was bringing a spare wheel and were making the most of the time by picking medicinal plants that grew in large numbers on both sides of the track. A tailwind, along with a slightly downhill gradient, propelled us for a couple more very easy kilometres before we picked a piece of grassland that for some reason ooked better than the infinite number of other potential campsites. We set up our tents, surrounded by marmot holes, then cooked delicious mutton dumplings that we had purchased from the last shop we had visited. After our main course I prepared the *Genghis Surprise*; probably the greatest desert ever eaten in Mongolia! It was a mixture of Snickers, wafer biscuits and chocolate biscuits, mashed up together and mixed with honey. As we finished our meal it started drizzling; confirmation that it was time for bed.

Herding a bull

Land of the blue skies

Puncture repair

Moving house (literally)

Meadows of wildflowers

An Eastern Buzzard (I think)

Day 11: The best camp
Distance travelled: 93.39 km

It is all too easy to forget that mankind is a part of nature, and not apart from it
- HRH the Price of Wales

The rain had continued for most of the night so the ground was damp, but fortunately it had stopped before we got up that morning. A cup of tea warmed us up as we sat on the marmot-infested, wildflower-covered prairie, preparing to set off across the steppe once again. The grass was very wet, making our shoes soggy as we crossed back to the trail. There were lots of parallel roads heading in the general direction of the next town that we would reach, named Tsagaan-Uul. Picking the least bumpy-looking, we crossed a couple of small passes on a very remote track, on which we saw only one other person all morning. He was a marmot hunter, who seemed to have been very successful already that day, since there were at least five carcasses on the back of his motorbike. We saw him carrying another back to the bike with an old wooden rifle slung over his back. He must have been an excellent shot.

Marmot hunting is common in Mongolia. It is sometimes practiced by nomads to hunt for food for their household and sometimes to sell the carcasses to others. Many Mongolians hunt marmots for a living, both for the meat and the fur, the latter being an important export for the country. The practice is frowned upon by many because marmots are plague carriers. However, the marmot hunters' traditional methods do protect against the hunting of infected animals. Traditionally, they wear a fully white outfit, although the guy we saw had a more traditional green deel on. The hunter wore a hat with long rabbit ears and held a *daluur*, which is a tassel, about 30 centimetres long made from a horse or yak tail attached to a small wooden handle. When hunting, the daluur is used to distract the marmot and cause it to sound its warning call, which gives away its position. If the marmot stops calling, the hunter shakes the rabbit ears, again to distract the marmot. This allows them to approach the marmot closely, within the distance of a rifle shot. If the marmot does not sound the warning call, this is a sign that it is infected with the plague, so the hunter will not shoot it. It is vitally important that the hunter has an excellent shot that kills the marmot instantly. If the animal is wounded, it will run back into its hole to die and so becomes very difficult to collect.

Traversing around a hill, we saw a few wooden buildings erected in the middle of nowhere, which turned out to be shepherds' huts, used in the winter to escape the freezing snow. A beautiful descent along a grassy valley led us into Tsagaan-Uul, where we had yet another portion of deep-fried buuz in a modern and very full restaurant. I changed 100 dollars for Mongolian tugrik at a local bank, then exited to find a local man riding around in circles on my bike. Phil had been waiting outside and reported that he had helped himself to a go on it without asking. This is completely normal behaviour in Mongolia! We resupplied at a well-stocked supermarket. Now that we were out of Western Mongolia, it was less important to carry large quantities of water since we would be riding next to rivers more regularly, in the much wetter, north-central part of the country.

On the way out of Tsagaan-Uul, we took a wrong turning en-route to the next town, named *Burenkhaan*. The riding was not particularly interesting that day, although the rolling hills through the continuing, seemingly endless grasslands were beautifully picturesque. After around an hour of afternoon riding, we realised that we were cycling along the wrong valley. We had taken the left fork in the track, rather than the right, which meant we were now cycling on a road that was not marked on the map. It didn't matter since it was heading in roughly the right direction. The only problem was that this new route would involve an additional climb over the large mountains separating our valley from the one we were supposed to be riding along. To pass the time as the miles rolled under our wheels, I told Phil the plot of the first Game of Thrones book, which kept us both entertained for an hour-or-so.

By mid-afternoon, we had reached the top of the pass that would put us back on to our intended route. The descent that followed was great fun; a twisting dirt track that led to a much larger, bumpier and rockier road along the valley floor. Another, identical looking grass-covered ridge of hills lay on the other side of the road, but we turned left at the bottom, heading east along the valley, which led to a small town, where we ordered a giant portion of buuz; a mistake as it was only five o'clock and we had more miles to cover. We had planned to turn north at this point, along a road that was marked on Google Maps, as the most direct route to the giant lake of Khövsgöl Nuur to the north. In the restaurant, however, we were told that it was not possible to pass that way, as a large, deep, uncrossable river was in the way. Perhaps the marked road was only used in winter, when the river would freeze over, or perhaps Google Maps was wrong. Either way, we needed to change our plan and the only other route available to us was the main road that led to Mörön, where there was a bridge over the Delgermörön Gol.

The final pass of the day led past gigantic red-grey crags that looked as though they would have hundreds of unknown climbing routes up them. We imagined coming back with ropes and being the first to ascend these cliffs. A large pickup truck descended the road we were climbing with an entire ger packed into the back. The driver waved cheerfully at us as we sweated up the climb. Finally reaching the giant ovoo at the top, we were treated to a stunning view of the wide Delgarmurin Gol, snaking across a giant plain. Both feeling the effect of eleven days of back-to-back cycling, we decided to treat ourselves to an early finish. Descending from the pass, we picked a point to leave the road and cycled directly down a mountain slope that was first rocky, then marshy, until it gave way to a flat field with metre-tall grass, which we crossed on our fatbikes, crushing the stalks beneath our wheels. It was difficult to see where we were going in the long grass but we kept our bearing, heading towards some large trees on the river bank. After a few minutes, we reached the river to find another contender for the best campsite of our trip. We planned to set up camp, then attempt some fishing, in what Phil informed me was one of the best fishing rivers in Mongolia.

Pushing our bikes onto the river bank, a soft grassy floor provided the perfect place to pitch the tents underneath an ancient looking deciduous tree. To the west, the evening sun highlighted the contours of five adjacent hills that gave way to the deep-blue, fast-flowing water of the Delgarmurin Gol. No human influence on the landscape was in sight and we were completely alone; our own private paradise. Soon, however, our home for the night was invaded by a herd of yaks. They stood in a group of around fifteen on the other side of the river, staring in our direction. There were a few giants in the herd as well as five calves who looked very young. To our surprise, one of the larger yaks stepped into the river and began to cross the fast-flowing water that almost reached its chin. The others followed, creating white water as the river flowed around their giant bodies. The power of the water must have made it incredibly difficult for the yaks to stay standing and showed us why we had been told that the river was impossible for us to cross. The yaks were managing it though and the first began the climb up to our river bank through gradually more and more shallow water until it emerged with water dripping from its shaggy coat as it stood looking rather comical on the sandy beach next to the flowing water. It turned around to watch the rest of the herd cross. The calves had now entered the water but were struggling. Their mothers stood downstream of them, providing support against the flow of the water and aiding their progress. It was slow going, but they were eventually successful and the whole herd managed to cross safely. Once on our side, they showed no interest whatsoever in us, passing by in search of the grass that was evidently so much tastier on this side of the river than it had been on the other. The grass is always greener...

By that time, we had set up camp and had washed in the river. Phil got out his fly-fishing rod and I set up my hook and line. We looked like complete amateurs as we stood on the river bank (and I suppose that we were). I cast my hook into the river and the weight got stuck on a rock, which ripped it off as I pulled it in. Phil's hook entered the water repeatedly as he moved it up and down, hoping for a bite. Unfortunately, neither of us saw a fish let along caught one. Phil read his guidebook again to read about the river's fishing potential and realised that he had misread its name. We were not camping on the side of a great fishing river after all! The water was far too fast flowing for our basic equipment and we conceded defeat. A couple of hours passed, during which we drank tea, cooked potatoes on a fire, read, caught up on diaries and enjoyed a well-earned rest. It was the perfect end to another memorable day in Mongolia.

Choose a road... any road

Delgermörön Gol

Yak crossing

Another stunning campsite

Day 12: It was going so well…
Distance travelled: 72.9 km

If a man fails seven times, he succeeds on the eighth
-Mongolian proverb

I woke up feeling great after two long evenings off the bike. After a quick breakfast at our perfect campsite, we packed up our kit and set off. This process now took about 30 minutes, which was considerably quicker than on our first morning It had taken me a few iterations to discover the best and most efficient use of space, within the differently shaped bikepacking bags I had fitted to my fatbike. I had now perfected the packing process. Leaving the river bend, we rode back through the long grass and found our way onto the main road, which followed the river for a few kilometres. A long pass followed, which I rode it as fast as I could, pushing hard and enjoying the challenge. It took about 15 minutes to reach the top and I could feel my stamina returning, as I was able to work hard all the way up the climb. After around a couple of weeks of daily cycling on a bike tour, there is usually a noticeable increase in fitness.

A short but fun descent to the small town of Burentogtokh brought us back down to the floodplain of the Delgermörön Gol. We were both getting rather bored of eating buuz in every restaurant but there wasn't much choice so we swallowed more deep-fried, greasy mutton then explored the town. A large fenced-off complex in the middle of town was deserted. It turned out to be a large school, which no pupils were currently attending because it was the summer holiday. During term-time however, the place would be transformed from a quiet and empty collection of buildings to a bustling noisy town. The school grounds had large dormitories with giant pipes connected to a central boiler, presumably used during the winter to keep the children warm when it was -40 degrees Celsius outside. After completing a lap of the school, we left the town, cycling on a long, straight and bumpy main road towards the large city of Mörön.

We passed across a wide flat plain, far enough away from the river that we couldn't see it, so there was nothing interesting to look at that afternoon, other than the odd sign that was counting down the kilometres to Mörön. We would be cycling for around 50 kilometres along this dull road, until we reached Mörön, so we had to find a way to entertain ourselves that afternoon. We spent an hour or so discussing James Bond films and theme tunes, deciding that Sean was clearly the best actor but it was a close-run thing between Piers and Roger for second. Goldeneye came out top of the film list and Diamonds are Forever, the best theme tune… boring miles!

Finally, we reached the final bend in the road, which would lead us to the bridge over the Delgermörön Gol and the final 12 kilometres of the day's cycle. We had made good time and were looking forward to a long afternoon off in the city, where we would have the chance to eat something that wasn't buuz. Then… CRACK… my entire bike juddered and my cranks started grinding before coming to a stop. They were completely locked up. I got off my bike to examine the damage, to find that it looked serious. Shards of metal were sticking out at all sorts of angles from my bottom bracket (the bearings that normally allow the cranks to rotate). One of the bearings had failed, but not gradually as would happen in 99.9 percent of bottom bracket failures, but instantly. Normally a bottom bracket will slowly fail and start making grinding noises as well as developing a bit of play. When I cycled around the world, I completed 14,379 miles on a single bottom bracket, which was loud and wobbly before I started the final leg across the continent of North America. It survived the final few thousand kilometres though, despite the wobble and noise getting worse and worse. The bottom bracket that I was currently using was about a year old, so I cursed myself for not having replaced it before travelling to Mongolia. Phil persuaded me that there was not a lot I could have done about it and it was a very unfortunate failure that should not have happened.

We were in trouble, being in the middle of a vast country in which the only place to buy modern bike components is its capital city, Ulaanbaatar. Discussing our options highlighted the magnitude of the problem. We were around 700 kilometres from Ulaanbaatar; a 1,400-kilometre round trip which would take at least two days. There was the option of flying from Mörön, but that would be an expensive choice and would also take two days to get there and back. It was incredibly unlikely that we would be able to find any replacement parts in Mörön and a bottom bracket is not the sort of component that you can easily bodge since it transmits so much torque to the rear wheel and needs to be able to withstand large pedalling forces in all directions. Having decided to travel light, neither of us had brought spare parts or even the tool we needed to remove the broken bottom bracket.

Whatever we decided to do involved getting to Mörön first, so we discussed the immediate plan. We could attempt to hitch a lift, we could walk, or Phil could go ahead for help. I was favouring the walking idea. 12 kilometres would take around three hours, compared to one on a bike, but at least this would mean that we would still be crossing the country without any assistance. Then I had a better idea. We rigged up a tow rope from Phil's bike, using a spare ratchet strap. Phil cycled for a while, with me holding on to the tow tope and steering my bike with one hand. When Phil wanted a rest, we swapped positions. We were able to travel at about nine kilometres per hour like this and within an hour and a half we were on the outskirts of Mörön, having received lots of wave and incredulous looks as we approached. Imagine the scene from the eyes of a local; two dirty Europeans, riding bikes with comically large wheels, one holding a nylon strap, being towed by the other! At least we could see the funny side.

On the outskirts of Mörön, I asked to borrow an eight-millimetre Allen key at a couple of petrol stations, which was what I needed to remove the cranks and examine the damage further. Neither had one, so we continued into the city, now pushing the bikes along a pavement. We were unsure what to do, thinking that it might be best to find a hotel then search for a bike shop on the off-chance they had the component that I needed. We passed a small medical centre, outside of which was locked a decent-looking mountain bike with some modern components. I went inside to the waiting room and tracked down the owner who was leaving anyway. She explained that the bike had been purchased in Ulaanbaatar and that there were no good bike shops in Mörön, but kept saying *"zakh, zakh"*. We had learnt that this word meant market when we had been in Ulaangom; the city we had visited on the other side of the Gobi Desert. She beckoned for us to follow and with no idea where she was taking us, we walked for twenty minutes or so, towards the centre of Mörön. At a crossroads, we clocked a large hotel that we could return to later if needed.

The very helpful lady led us to a car garage, in which a friend of hers worked, before cheerfully waving at us and disappearing. I explained the problem to a group of mechanics who instantly stopped working on the various cars that they had in pieces, to see what on Earth we wanted. With a large reassuring smile, a young mechanic took my bike and wheeled it to a pillar, which he leaned it against. Two minutes later, he had used an Allen key to remove the cranks, a large grip wrench to take out the bottom bracket and the entire mechanism was dismantled: problem one solved! This was rather impressive since he had almost certainly never seen this sort of component before. The destroyed bearing was removed and the mechanics looked concerned, shaking their heads at the extent of the damage. The young mechanic beckoned me to follow him. Phil said he would stay with the bikes and our kit so I left everything with him and followed the mechanic. The mechanic grabbed the dismantled components and spoke to a friend outside the garage who drove us to the market that was ten minutes away.

First stop was a bearing shop, on the floor of which, two men in overalls slept. We woke them up and the mechanic showed them the damaged bearing as well as the "cup", which is a piece of metal that holds the bearing in place and threads into the bike frame. After ten minutes of searching through the endless piles of bearings, we were told that they had nothing that could help. The problem I had was that a bike bearing is very thin precision component. It is not designed to withstand large forces in comparison to motorised vehicles. All the parts in the car and motorbike shops were heavy duty and larger, so would not fit. I needed a bearing with very small rolling balls, with an internal diameter that was much larger in comparison to its outer diameter than is the case in motorbike bearings.

We moved on to a large, covered market area, visiting a few bike shops with no success. If I had been riding a bike from the nineties, I would have had a vast array of parts to choose from but nothing here would fit onto my fatbike. A couple more bearing shops had no parts either, so in a desperate final attempt, we went back to the first one. The mechanic and I both searched for bearings this time and eventually I found something that looked as though it might work. It had the same inner diameter as the broken bearing and so the crank axle fitted perfectly though the middle of it. The bearing shop owner found the rest of the bearing and sold it to the mechanic who I would pay back later. We were driven back to the garage where Phil sat reading the guidebook. It was soon clear that the bearing would not fit into the bottom bracket tube in the bike frame. The inner raceway (a steel cylinder) did slot very nicely into the bottom bracket cup though, so we assembled the components we had, put it all together and did it up. The cranks would not spin at all because it was clamped together too tightly, so we took the system apart again and removed a spacer, which allowed it to loosen up. Amazingly the cranks spun round, with only a little additional friction slowing them down. The driveside bearing did not move at all, but the cranks spun round inside the inner cylinder of the bearing we had bought in the market. This would eventually cause the crank axle to wear down because it is made from a softer metal that than the hard bearing steel but if I kept it well lubricated, perhaps it would last another couple of weeks. My PhD on wind turbine gearbox bearings was coming in useful!

Eternally grateful for all the help, I gave the mechanic 20,000 tugrik, which is about ten dollars. He was very pleased with the tip since when I asked how much I owed him, he didn't want anything. We were unsure of how long the bodge would hold for but it got us around the corner to the hotel we had seen earlier, named 50° 100° hotel, referring to its latitude north and longitude east. The hotel was excellent and by far the best we had been to in Mongolia. The rooms were spotless, with a television that had a channel showing the Rio Olympics. After sorting our equipment and having a wash we headed to the restaurant where we ate fried beef alongside an ice-cold beer. I was very optimistic about the fix and thought it would probably hold for a few days. Perhaps if we could keep bodging it, the problem would not affect our trip.

The incredibly helpful mechanic

Investigating the problem

Day 13: Motorbike bearing bodge

Distance travelled: 86.8 km

No problem is insurmountable. With a little courage, teamwork and determination a person can overcome anything.
- B. Dodge

I didn't sleep well, worrying about the broken bottom bracket and turning ideas over in my head. Perhaps there was a better way to setup the bodge; maybe I should get a friend from home to post a new component out; maybe I should hitch to Ulaanbaatar while we were in a city. When I woke up in the morning it was clear that the best thing to do was to test it out and hope that it would survive. We ate breakfast, which included egg, sausage, fried bread and strangely; chicken soup. After packing up the bags, we headed back to the bikes where I tested my cranks again. They were still quite stiff and there was no play at all in the *bearings*, so I thought it may be a good idea to remove another spacer to give them more room to rotate.

We left the city via our legendary mechanic friends who quickly took the spacer out for us then waved farewell once more. Cycling north out of Mörön felt great. I had entered the city on a crippled bike but was leaving it on a working one. It was now performing ell too and it was barely noticeable that anything was wrong. The pedals were slightly stiffer than usual but this didn't really affect my speed, or the effort that I needed to put into pedalling the bike. Usefully it turned out that a new tarmac road had been built linking Mörön with the southern shore of Khovsgul Nuur, the lake we would reach the following day. We bought some food from a small shop on the way out of Mörön, then were riding through quiet countryside once more, cycling uphill towards the lake that lies at an altitude of 1,645 metres.

I enjoyed the long climb up the hill that morning and cycled in a lower gear than normal to reduce the force on the bottom bracket, although my legs spun round more quickly. At around lunchtime we reached the top of a pass at an altitude of 1,850 metres. It was the first touristy place we had seen in Mongolia and it reminded me of some of the passes that I had crossed in the Indian Himalayas on my last long cycle tour. On top of the pass were a few souvenir shops, lots of restaurants and a Shaman Museum inside a ger. Outside the "museum" were the first reindeer I had ever seen, tall and strong with gigantic tree-like antlers. The area to the west of Khövsgöl Nuur is the centre of the Mongolian Shamanist religion, where it has been practiced since before the age of recorded history. The

95

religion involves the worship of the Tngri (Gods) and particularly the highest Tenger (the God of Heaven). Genghis Khan is considered, by Shamans, to have been a human embodiment of the Tenger. One division of Mongolian Shamanism worship at Ovoos, which to them are sacrificial altars thought to be representations of the various gods. Mongolian shamanism is a system that includes medicine, religion and worshiping nature and ancestors. Ancestral worship includes rituals used to communicate with the spirit world, where shamans enter a trancelike state during which they practice divination and healing. Unfortunately, we didn't have enough time to detour through this region, but over the next few days we saw many examples of its influence on the area we were travelling through, including the practice of ovoo worship.

We decided not to stop at any of the touristy tents and descended a short distance from the pass to a large plain where we stopped, having cycled 40 kilometres that morning. As we ate, a large herd of camels passed us, all the normal sandy-brown colour apart from one which was snow-white. One small pass later we were both bored of cycling on the road. We had pumped our tyres up to around 25 psi, which is very hard for a fatbike. It did mean that the fatbikes were working well on the tarmac with very little drag compared to when the tyres were softer. Phil was very tired and this, combined with boredom, was causing him to fall asleep on his bike as we freewheeled downhill. We stopped to look at a map and noticed that there was a small river that flowed from the lake close to our road. A few kilometres upstream it passed through a small village, which was connected to the main road by a dirt track. Both of us needed a change of scene so we left the road to see if we could find our way to the village off-road.

A narrow motorbike track left the road, heading down a small valley towards the river and led to a large pasture that was full of sheep, cattle and goats. There must have been at least 500 animals grazing on the plain. The pasture was situated between the river and some small cliffs, which goats had climbed. Many stood on high ledges peering down at the grassland below. We followed the motorbike track, which was a narrow dirt path that followed the base of the cliffs. Soon the path intersected the Egiin River, the crystal-clear outlet of Khövsgöl Nuur that we were edging closer and closer towards. Pine trees covered the hillside on the other side of the river and our path soon entered a small woodland, leaving the pasture behind. The path through the woods was a perfect section of mountain biking singletrack that was probably formed by the footfall of animals. The track wove in and out of the trees, up and down small mounds, getting funnelled between the river and the cliffs, which were approaching one another. A strong smell of pine hung in the perfectly fresh country air. Eventually the path became overgrown and we were forced to push our bikes through the thick undergrowth until we reached a dead-end. The cliff and the river had met and there was no way of continuing. The river flowed quickly around the outside of a bend, the large cliffs towering above the water.

Our only options were to attempt to cross the river or to turn back. We left the bikes on the river bank and started wading through the water to find a good place to cross. It was not possible directly across from the river bend because the water was too deep and fast flowing. Phil found a route a few metres downstream, where the river was slightly wider and shallower. It was still deep however and the water flowed quickly. Wading through the river to test the crossing was difficult enough and on the far bank was deep, squishy mud that we sunk into when we stepped through it. Happy that it was possible to cross we took Phil's bike across first lifting one side each above the level of the water so that Phil's panniers didn't get wet. Successfully across the water, we left Phil's bike and returned to mine carrying it across. On the second crossing I noticed the carcass of a cow that was lying in the shallows near the far bank; a reminder not to drink water from large rivers.

With wet feet, we cycled around the river bend and saw the small village, now on the opposite bank. After a few hundred metres we needed to cross back. The second crossing was easier. We could walk our bikes across by lifting them at waist height. As we entered the village, we were buzzing after our little adventure along the Egiin Gol. It had certainly been more interesting than the road route. A quick ice cream at a small village shop refreshed us, then we rolled another 20 kilometres along the main road until it intersected the river once more. At this point there was a perfectly flat grassy field next to the riverbank. After cycling a few hundred metres upstream to put some distance between us and the road, we pitched the tents on another beautifully scenic campsite.

We cooked dinner as the sky darkened. A huge thunderstorm was forming to the west, as the light level became lower and lower with the thickening cloud. The horizon was an intimidating sight as the temperature dropped and the wind picked up. Huge vultures circled around in the sky at a great height, travelling at speed but looking as though they were putting in no effort whatsoever as they glided over their territory. We quickly cooked dinner, which we ate in Phil's tent when the heavens opened. The torrential rain continued for an hour and a half and Phil's tent was still leaking, so a puddle began to form near the back of his groundsheet. We ate, wrote diaries, looked through some photos of the last few days and drank tea as the tents were tested by the howling gale outside. The ground shock every time there was a clap of thunder and the sky flashed with lightning. Camping in a thunderstorm is not the most comfortable experience.

After the rain stopped we exited Phil's tent. It turned out that a campervan had pulled up during the storm. We walked over and were greeted by Krysten and Bart, a Dutch couple who were travelling through Mongolia together. They put up a folding table and chairs and offered us a cup of coffee as we discussed our trips. Krysten had flown out to meet Bart a week ago, but before that, Bart had driven his Lada four-by-four all the way to Mongolia from the Netherlands. He was very interesting, being completely eccentric. Bart is an artist who specialises in steel sculptures. He had made a giant steel horse that stood on a trailer, which he had towed from his home in the Netherlands to the annual Nadaam festival in Ulaanbaatar. He was aiming to sell the horse to a collector in Ulaanbaatar and apparently had a potential buyer. His route was similar to the route that I took on my cycle ride around the world. He had also taken the Caspian Sea Ferry from Baku in Azerbaijan, to Aktau in Kazakhstan. On the crossing his friend and cameraman had used a drone to capture some amazing footage of the old Soviet ferry crossing the Caspian Sea. Bart had also loved Georgia, which is possibly the best country I have ever visited (although Mongolia may well be taking that crown).

I told Bart and Krysten about my broken bottom bracket. They told me that they had met a group of cyclists who were taking part in the inaugural mountain bike race around Khövsgöl Nuur, starting the following morning. Apparently, a British guy named Joe had set it up with the help of a financial backer from Ulaanbaatar. The event was sponsored by Merida, a giant Chinese mountain bike manufacturer. This was surely an opportunity to try to get hold of the spare parts I needed. We decided to get up very early the next day to attempt to catch the cyclists before the race left, since we would need to cycle 20 kilometres before nine o'clock in the morning.

Reindeer at the "Shamen Museum"

Our detour away from the main road

Finding new trails

Camping on the Elgin Gol near to Khövsgöl Nuur

Day 14: Khövsgöl Nuur

Distance travelled: 24 km

Mountains are the beginning and end of all natural scenery
- John Ruskin

We were ready to leave by seven o'clock. Bart came over to us in nothing but his y-fronts to tell us that he hadn't been able to get in touch with Joe regarding the bottom bracket. He gave us directions to the start-line of the mountain bike race, which sounded easy to find being just off the main road. We departed our campsite and cycled the non-eventful 20-kilometre stretch to Khatgal. There is normally a park fee to enter Khövsgöl Nuur National Park but it was too early for the cesk to be manned so we were unable to pay it. I had been expecting Khatgal to be touristy, but I was surprised how much of a tourist hotspot it was with large supermarkets, restaurants and hundreds of gers that could be rented at various ger camps. It didn't take us long to find Joe and the start point of the Khövsgöl Mountain Bike Challenge. As we approached he came over to talk to us, very interested in our journey. We asked him about the race. There were ten competitors or the ride, which would take them around the lake on a 400-kilometre journey over seven days. It was notionally a race, but really it was about completing the ride. Competitors were supported by a boat that would travel around the lake. The organisers on the boat would take camping equipment and spare parts to the riders, as well as providing backup and first aid if required. It was a great event.

I soon asked the vital question; *was there a spare bottom bracket that I could buy from them*? Unfortunately, nobody had one and it was confirmed that there were no bike shops in our close vicinity. The only other bike shop that Joe knew of in Mongolia was in the city of Tserterleg about 600 kilometres south of us, which was obviously not an option either. I was stuck with my bodged bottom bracket that had already developed quite a bit of play. Joe had a quick go on each of the fat bikes, announced that he was going to buy one, and then lined up on the start line with the other competitors. We were asked to stand on the start line too for a photograph and then the "*grand depart*". A few motivational words in Mongolian followed before cheering from the competitors raised the excitement, and then a lady approached each bike and spooned a ladleful of milk onto each of our front wheels. Milk sprinkling is a long-standing tradition in Mongolia, which often takes place before a traveller departs on a long journey. A small amount of milk is poured on an object to ask the Gods for a blessing. Everyone present is required to think *good thoughts* to honour the Gods of fertility and protection. It is believed that this tradition helps the traveller to return home safely.

After the race had begun, we cycled back towards the centre of Khatgal and found an acceptable looking ger camp. There was a large common room, hot showers and even a Wi-Fi connection. It was also right next to what Bart had told us was the best restaurant in town. We unloaded our stuff into one of the gers, inside of which were three beds, a table and a sofa. I then dismantled my broken bottom bracket once again to find that a lot of damage had already been caused to the cup that was holding the new bearing. I cleaned it out and put in the old bearing's outer cylinder, inserted some of the roller balls that I had saved, then inserted the new inner cylinder along with a lot of grease that I had brought in my toolkit. I would need to buy some more when possible as it was running low. The new fix was better as the old bearing outer cylinder fitted perfectly into the cup and the new inner sat nicely against it. If the crank bolt was left a bit loose the bearing even rotated. When done up tightly, the cranks spun in the inner cylinder as the bearing was jammed by the bolt's tension. This wasn't a problem as the cranks still span round without too much drag. My bike was ready to continue but I had no idea how long it would last. The next section of our ride would be very remote so the idea of breaking down in the middle of nowhere was rather concerning. We would have to risk it though and there was nothing to be done about it that day. Instead we planned to explore the town and the lake.

We first went to a supermarket to buy supplies for the next leg of the journey, including a small bottle of sunflower oil, which would work as a lubricant for my cranks until we could find some proper grease. There was a working ATM in one of the shops, so we extracted some much-needed cash as we were running low and none of the banks seemed to want to exchange dollars. Passing several *Karaoke Bars* we went to a restaurant for a real coffee, which was a treat since it was not cheap! Mongolians do not seem to drink coffee and proper beans are a luxury. Heading down to the lakeside we stopped for a tasty kebab at a fast food van, thinking that this town couldn't be any more different from the vast steppe that we had been crossing for the last two weeks.

Known as the Blue Pearl of Mongolia, Lake Khövsgöl is 136-kilometres long, surrounded by mountains and formed by the same tectonic process as Siberia's famous Lake Baikal, into which it drains via the Selenge River. Up to 262 metres deep, it contains between one and two percent of the world's freshwater! It is full of fish, including sturgeon, and the surrounding countryside is home to bear, moose, wolverines and ibex. On the lakeside was a port, with a few large boats. We had a quick look around a visitor centre, which contained some extremely old diving equipment. The old kit was incredibly heavy and relied on two people operating an air-pump to supply a very trusting diver via a long pipe. Bus-loads of Mongolian tourists from Ulaanbaatar had come to Khövsgöl Nuur to experience the scenery. You could spot someone from the capital a mile off. They were dressed in fashionable western-style clothes, drove fancy cars and seemed to be much more flustered and in a rush than their rural countrymen.

Mongolia is the second largest landlocked country in the world after Kazakhstan, although Kazakhstan has a coastline along the giant inland lake, the Caspian Sea, which it shares with Russia, Georgia, Azerbaijan, Iran and Turkmenistan. Unlike Mongolia these countries operate large international ferries and trading ships. Mongolia has no coastline at all so there are no large boats in the country other than those on lakes. It is likely that the tourist ferry at Khatgal, the Sukhbaatar, is the largest boat in Mongolia, since Khövsgöl Nuur is its largest lake other than Uvs Nuur. Uvs Nuur however, has no water-based transport on it as it is very shallow and highly saline with very few edible fish. The Mongolian tourists clearly thought that travelling by boat was a novel experience. On-board there was a karaoke competition, where people from the audience could volunteer to sing Mongolian pop songs as the ferry steered its way across the beautiful and otherwise perfectly peaceful lake.

After a couple of beers, two smoked fish and far too much Mongolian karaoke, the ship docked at Khatgal once more. We tried and failed to hitch a lift to our ger camp, so walked for about half an hour until we arrived back there, planning to sort ourselves out for the next leg of the trip. Unfortunately, the owner of the ger camp had disappeared with no warning, so we were unable to use the locked bathroom facilities or the common room and Wi-Fi. There was a smelly long-drop toilet at the back of the field on which the ger camp was set up but that was not quite what we had paid for! After sorting out our kit, reading up on the next leg in our guidebooks, plugging in various electronic devices to charge and packing up what we could, it was dinner time and there was still no shower. Finally, the owner returned saying that he had been on a walk in the hills with his family. Maybe that is how things work here! We both had a quick shower, which we were informed cost another 5,000 tugrik (3 dollars) each, then went for dinner at the Chingghis Restaurant next door to the camp. They sold steak there. We both ordered one and enjoyed what was an unusually delicious meal in comparison to our usual fare. After dinner we had an early night, ready for the next section of our trip. We planned to have a leisurely ride the following day so that we could enjoy camping on the lake shore before turning east once more, into the remote pine forested hills that lie next to the great lake.

The start of the Khövsgöl Mountain Bike Challenge

The lake trip on Khövsgöl Nuur

Day 15: Camping on Khövsgöl Nuur
Distance travelled: 39.04 km

There are men who walk through the woods and see no trees
- Mongolian proverb

With our electrical equipment fully charged and our kit dry, we set off, looking forward to an easy relaxing day. Our *bed and breakfast* ger camp turned out not to offer breakfast, so we stopped off at the Chingghis restaurant again where we enjoyed bacon and eggs; a wonderful start to the day! We had noticed many more Toyata Prius hybrids throughout the town of Khatgal as well as on many of the surrounding roads that we had cycled along. Bart had told us that these cars had become so popular in Mongolia because the government heavily subsidise hybrids to counter the dangerously elevated levels of pollution in Ulaanbaatar each winter. At the restaurant, we met a girl from Ireland, who was on her way home, travelling overland from Shanghai. She was planning to catch the Trans-Siberian railway to Moscow for the next leg of her trip and like us, had loved Mongolia so far.

Leaving Khatgal via another supermarket, we needed to backtrack a few kilometres along the main road from Mörön. At the bottom of the lake there is a bridge where it narrows and drains into the Egiin River. We turned off the main road and crossed the bridge, which led to a dirt track that continues all the way to Khankh on the Russian border. This border crossing is closed to third-party nationals so was no use to us. It is used widely in the long winter for fuel deliveries from Russia when Khövsgöl Nuur freezes to a depth of over one metre. The thick ice is strong enough for fuel trucks from Russia to drive on the surface of the lake, creating a perfectly flat road linking Mongolia to Russia. Our road was not flat however. The dirt track was bumpy, sandy and had lots of deep puddles from the storm that we had been caught in two nights ago. The road passed though stunning scenery, climbing a small pass that left behind wide grassy pastures, then entering a thick natural pine forest on a steeper, rockier track. Passing a Toyota Prius inching its way down the track and driven by a very fashionably dressed young lady, highlighted again what a strange choice of car it is for so many wealthy Mongolians!

Two motorcyclists pulled over for a chat. They were a couple; the man was Australian and the woman, German. We were very interested to hear that they had come along the same road that we planned to take and encouraged to hear that it was passable. We were less pleased to hear their stories of swarms of

105

mosquitoes, barely crossable rivers and very difficult road surfaces. They had decent motorbikes, so if they had struggled it would be a difficult route for us to take. In fact they both looked thoroughly miserable and exhausted. They had nothing good to say about their experience and complained a lot about a large music festival that was happening on the lake shore a few kilometres to the north. After complaining about how awful their $13 per day hire bikes were, they headed off to Khatgal, which they weren't looking forward to at all since it was a "*tourist trap with awful accommodation*". As they left we looked at each other dumbfounded! We couldn't believe that they had not enjoyed anything about their trip in Mongolia. Looking around at the stunning scenery reminded that we were, in fact, in one of the most beautiful corners of one of the most beautiful countries in the world.

Continuing, we discussed the importance of a certain personality type for self-supported adventure holidays. I thought myself very lucky that Phil was so easy-going and considered that it was remarkable that the two of us had spent a total of around three months of our lives travelling together on bikes, without a single disagreement or argument. Soon we were passing the turn-off to the music festival, which seemed to be winding down but looked to have been surprisingly large, judging by the gazebos and the number of vehicles parked on the open grasslands by the lakeside. Herds of yaks grazed all around us alongside the ever-present goats and sheep. Our road crossed a few small rivers, which were not deep enough to get our feet wet, and led us to a gentle climb and a completely unmarked junction with the road that would take us to the small town of Chandmani-Öndör. This was the most northern point of the lakeside road that we would reach, since the following day we would be heading east once more. It would have been a criminal offence to pass Khövsgöl Nuur without having spent a night camping on its shore, so we turned west instead. After a kilometre and a half of riding across open grassland, we reached a gem of a campsite.

With the vast, open, deep-blue lake water stretching out to the north and the south and the beautiful forested mountains lining the western shore on the horizon, our campsite was situated in an epic, quiet, peaceful and almost impossibly scenic spot. We pitched the tents in a pine forest above a stony beach, completely isolated from the rest of the world. It was just three o'clock in the afternoon and the whole evening was ahead of us, seemingly an infinite time for us to relax and enjoy the beauty of the place. After setting up camp we swam and washed in the surprisingly warm water, then collected firewood. We sat on the beach for a long time, chatting, drinking tea, planning our route for the rest of the trip and discussing how pleased we were with the bottom bracket bodge. If it could just survive for a few hundred more kilometres, we would be rather pleased with our on-the-road mechanical skills!

On the far shoreline we could see many white dots; the ever-present and comforting sight of gers. Giant hawks swooped over the lake, possibly looking for one of the many fish that make Khövsgöl Nuur a famous fisherman's paradise. We ate rice with fresh vegetables from the well-stocked supermarkets of Khatgal and drank three rounds of tea made from the lake water, which is apparently potable. Feeling incredibly relaxed, we went to bed both excited for our adventure to continue.

In bed that night I read our guidebook, including the legend of Khövsgöl Nuur. According to folklore the lake was formed as follows: *In ancient times, an old lady lived with her two daughters in a deep valley within Mongolia's northern mountains. She was a goat herder and each day, her daughters took the goats to a spring at the bottom of the valley. They removed a lid that covered the spring, allowing the water to flow out so that the goats could drink, but forgot to replace it. The spring overflowed all night and the next morning, the old women awoke to see that the valley was filled with water. She was very angry but also incredibly upset, so she cut the top off a nearby mountain and put it on top of the spring to stop the flow of water. She was too late though, since the lake had already formed. The mountain-top formed an island in the lake, which is now called Modon Huui (meaning "the lake's tree covered navel") and the flat-topped mountain that is missing its summit is called Orundush (meaning "the blacksmith's anvil").*

The lakeside road

Approaching Khövsgöl Nuur

Camping at Khövsgöl Nuur

An evening swim

Day 16: Off the beaten track

Distance travelled: 81.03 km

One arrow alone can be easily broken but many arrows are indestructible.
- Genghis Khan

A damp drizzly start to the day resulted in us having breakfast in Phil's tent. Our breakfasts were not usually very exciting; today's being Nutella, bread and bland biscuits. Packing up our campsite was now becoming second nature, so it took just a few minutes to load up the bikes and depart the beautiful lakeside. Riding back up the hill we discussed what laid ahead, having both looked at maps that morning. We were still using our phones to navigate most of the time, using the brilliant free app (Viewranger). I had the opensource map of our route downloaded onto my phone and Phil had satellite images on his. Navigation of the upcoming section of our ride would be perhaps the most difficult, since there were no major roads, lots of rivers to cross and large pine forests covering the hillsides, making the satellite images difficult to follow as the tracks were hidden.

We had decided to attempt to cycle through a remote area of the country to the east of Khövsgöl Nuur, heading towards the town of Chandmani-Öndör. This area is very sparsely populated, with only around 3000 inhabitants in 4,500 square kilometres. Reaching the main track that headed from Khatgal to the Russian border, we looked for the junction with the road heading east. We found it a few hundred metres up the hill. The track followed a boundary between a pine-clad hillside and a wildflower meadow and appeared to be very infrequently used, since grass and wildflowers grew in the two shallow ruts along which vehicle wheels rolled. Cycling parallel to each other, one of us in each rut, we climbed a short distance to a pass where the road entered the pine-scented forest. This very small bank was all that stopped Khosvgol Nuur from flowing into the large area of lower-lying land below. It is unusual for such a large lake to be contained in a high drainage basin surrounded by much lower lying land. This was good news for us though, because ahead lay a long fast descent to the river valley below. After the ovoo on the top of the pass, the track descended steeply on a loose stony surface until it left the thick pine forest again, turning back into a grassy track across a wildflower meadow between forested hillsides. The track continued downhill along a river valley before crossing a wide floodplain. The river had no name on our maps, but it was a significant tributary of the giant Selenge River, and it would lead us to Chandmani-Öndör. Over the course of that day, we slowly descended 800 metres along the river. The scenery was incredible. It looked more like Switzerland than the Mongolia we had experienced so far. People were not living in gers, but large log cabins, thanks to the plentiful supply of building material growing in the giant forests. The sun was shining once more, reflecting off glistening blue streams and rivers that joined the large tributary we were following. We regularly had to cross small streams and Phil was not having the best day on that front! On four occasions, he got stuck in the middle of the river crossings, having to put a foot down in the water and getting his feet wet. I lost no time in telling Phil that my feet were perfectly dry each time. Although the gradient was not steep enough for us to freewheel, it did help push us along slightly faster than normal, so we made excellent progress over the difficult terrain. We followed the river as it cut its way through the surrounding mountains, first north, then east, then south as it approached Chandmani-Öndör, all the while on the lovely, well-surfaced riverside path.

I had almost forgotten that my bike still had a significant mechanical problem, until the bottom bracket started wobbling again. I dismounted and investigated the problem. It looked as though the aluminium "cup" that was holding the "new" motorbike bearing was slowly wearing down. As the surface was rubbed away, the bearing had more room to wobble and to let dirt in. I very carefully dismantled the bottom bracket again. It was critical that I didn't break any components further, or lose any of the parts in the long grass. I cleaned the separate roller balls, as well as the metal surfaces, with toilet paper, then covered the components in vegetable oil before reassembling it with another bottom bracket spacer in an attempt to more tightly compress the bearing. It worked well and although the cranks were slightly stiffer than they should have been, they span round easily, made no noise and no longer wobbled. I was good to continue.

By mid-afternoon we were approaching Chandmani-Öndör from the north. The river was now wide and deep, but fortunately there was a footbridge that we were able to cross on our bikes. The town was beautiful, again constructed from pine trees, giving the place an alpine feel. We entered the town to the usual incredulous looks from the locals who were fascinated by our giant tyres! Heading straight for a café, we ordered mutton and noodle soup. I read about the town, finding out that its most famous historical inhabitant, Alan Goa. She was a direct ancestor of Genghis Khan, preceding him by ten generations and is a Mongolian heroin, partly responsible for the deep respect of women in this country both now and historically. Alan is a woman's name in Mongolian, and Goa means "*the beauty*". Alan is said to have had two sons with her husband, but three more after he died. The two eldest sons were deeply suspicious that their three younger half-brothers were fathered by a servant, so Alan sat them down for a meal. She gave each son an arrow and told them to break it, which they did easily. She then passed round a bundle of five arrows and asked them to break the bundle, which they could not do. She told the sons that they must stick together like the five arrows, since separately they could be broken, but together they could not be harmed.

After eating, we visited the two banks in the town, but neither would exchange dollars for tugrik. We had been reliant on being able to exchange money here and cursed ourselves for not getting more in Khatgal. We had the equivalent of around seven dollars left but had no food. A very frugal shopping trip allowed us to restock on bland boring snacks, which would get us to the next town, but no further. We desperately needed to exchange money there. Bidding farewell to the crowd that had developed around us, we continued due south on a well-used road. The road followed a wide floodplain to the east of the river, which had five large tributary crossings. Phil got wet feet again and they had been drying out! I found this very funny. It was very hot and humid that afternoon, partly due to the overcast weather conditions, but also partly due to the lower elevation. The floodplain widened giving way to a vast grassy meadow, in which stood a large statue of Alan Goa, complete with her five arrows. Offerings had been presented to her, including curd, milk, prayer flags and real arrows. This wide plain had recently hosted a large Nadaam festival in which wrestlers, archers and horse riders had competed for the right to represent the region at the national games in Ulanbaatar.

In both the regional and national Nadaam festivals, athletes compete in the three "*manly*" sports, which captivate villagers from all over the country. The first is horse racing, which is very different from the races that we are used to in the UK. Mongolian horse racing takes place over a much greater distance of at least 15 kilometres and the horses are prized for their endurance. They are generally much smaller and leaner than their Western cousins, but are much more capable over long distances. The second is wrestling, which is the Mongolian national sport and has been since the days of Genghis Khan, who considered the sport to be an important way to keep his soldiers fit and combat ready. The third is archery. Competitors fire at targets a long distance away; 75 metres for men and 65 metres for women. Mongolian archers wear the deel and leather sleeves up to their elbow to ensure that the fabric does not get in the way of the shot.

We looked at the remains of the regional Nadaam festival, which included a horse racing track, on which there were thousands of hoof-prints, some archery targets still constructed, the scaffolding that must have supported a stand for spectators and a circular area of worn grass, which must have been where the wrestling took place. It was clearly a large and very popular event amongst the local villagers. We continued south in the early evening, now looking for a place to camp, and passed a large animal skin stretched out on a metal frame and drying in the sun. Would it be used for clothing, for part of a ger, or as a rug?

The track approached the river again, which looked to be a beautiful place to stay for the night. The river had split into a few separate branches. Taking our shoes off, we carried our equipment and bikes across the first river channel, where there was a lovely grassy area on which we decided to camp. Next to this was a sandy beach on the river bank and a large pool which was linked to the river, but with no current so had been heated up by the sun. It would be perfect for a bath. There were trees and plenty of dry firewood. Eagles swooped across the plain and herds of cows and horses moved along the river. Unfortunately, the sky was darkening. We had a wash, collected firewood and cooked dinner as the storm approached. Across the plain we watched spectacular forked lightning striking the mountains as thunder shook the ground. The epic sky loomed above the plain and giant cumulonimbus clouds shrank the normally epic Mongolians landscape to relative insignificance. Fortunately, we seemed to be camping right on the edge of the storm. The rain had not hit us, although we could see it falling not far away. The wind had picked up, but we stayed outside watching the awesome force of nature while drinking a cup of tea. After a wash, dinner and more tea, we went to bed, thankful that the storm had missed us.

The track leading into the wilderness

Bottom bracket maintenance was becoming more and more regular

A typical dwelling in areas of Mongolia with access to pine forests

Crossing a bridge to Chandmani-Öndör

"Veitch's Blue" globe thistle

Campsite near the recent Nadaam festival

Day 17: Trails, trails, trails

Distance travelled: 80.54 km

While horse is strong, travel to see places
- Mongolian proverb

The greener, more fertile landscapes of northern Mongolia are markedly different from the drier steppes of the western part of the country. The change in scenery kept our adventure interesting, since the landscape had become more varied, and the wildlife and vegetation different. Unsurprisingly, this change in climate came with a change in the weather and having experienced almost no rain in Western Mongolia, we were now seeing daily rainstorms and consistently cloudy skies. The morning of day 17 was no different as we woke up to light drizzle falling on the canvas of our tents. Fortunately, the light rain didn't last long, so we sat on the river bank to cook breakfast. Phil's temperamental petrol stove was not working again. He had dismantled it and cleaned it out a few times, but couldn't get it burning. Instead, I made a fire while Phil continued trying to fix the stove. I finally got the fire burning, which had been difficult because the wood was wet. I put a pan on the fire and started boiling water for the tea. Phil managed to unblock the stove and also started boiling water for tea. We had two pans of tea that morning.

After packing up camp, we needed to lift our stuff across the river again. The crossing was straightforward and once on the other side, we pushed across an area of ground with large cobbles and boulders until we reached the track again. While making our final preparations before setting off for the day, Phil noticed that he didn't have his gloves. One regular and annoying occurrence when cycle touring is packing something into a bag that you need that day. Everyone who has been on a long tour will have done this at some point. The other annoying part of this experience is that in general, you will have absolutely no idea where the vital piece of equipment is located within your luggage. Phil's gloves were nowhere to be seen in his front bag, nor in his left pannier, nor in his right. They weren't in his sleeping bag and they had not ended up in any of my bags. He then remembered that they had been balanced on his bike before crossing the river. We turned back to the river, searching for the gloves. After 20 minutes of searching, Phil found one of them back on the other side of the river. After about an hour had passed, we gave up, which was a shame because the gloves were good ones; a present from Phil's brother Anthony. Preparing to leave, I looked down at Phil's bike and saw the missing glove stuck between the bike rack and the bike tyre. It was wedged there and had somehow clung on all this time. Phil was extremely pleased at the point of departure that day, wearing both of his cycling gloves, but with wet feet once again, since he had waded through the river so many times! I reminded him that mine were dry...

We soon turned east out of the valley, beginning a climb up another track that followed a small mountain stream. The ride up the pass was wonderful, climbing through a silent pine forest. The forest felt very old, with no sign of any human influence other than the narrow track. There were clearings in the forest, a few of which, our track bypassed. These were islands of life in which the sun shone on the ground, enabling beautiful, deep blue wildflowers to grow next to long grasses that bees buzzed around. Soon, the remote track became even more so. A thin, foot-wide path peeled off the main jeep track and remained separate from the main track for a couple of kilometres, climbing along the opposite side of the small mountain stream. The track had been formed by motorbikes looking for a more direct path through the forest. It would not have been out of place in a purpose-built mountain bike trail centre. The track flowed from one interesting feature to the next, weaving around trees, climbing over roots and rocks, crossing a stream, before descending and climbing up the undulating terrain. Regular use meant that the base of the track was solid to ride on and that banked corners had formed. This was possibly the best cycling of the whole trip, rivalling the trails that we had so enjoyed between Tes and Bayantes.

Although the riding was brilliant, we were both tiring and were low on energy. We needed a sugar boost and all we had left were a few stale biscuits. Our meagre food supplies and lack of cash to replace them were concerning. After few biscuits we were ready to push on for the top of the pass that separated us from, hopefully, our next decent meal. The track left the forest and crossed more pastures and streams as we climbed higher and higher on a now wet and slippery jeep track. Finally, we saw a tall and sinister looking ovoo ahead, signalling the mountain pass. It was constructed from long pine branches from which were hung many pieces of blue cloth. It would not have looked out of place in a horror film about witchcraft. On the centre of the ovoo were sheep skulls and animal horns, as well as a few wooden boxes and ornaments. Other offerings included cheese, bread and milk in plastic bottles. Despite its sinister look, it was a comforting sight and the belief of the local people that these ovoos helped protect them on their journey encouraged me to observe it with a degree of reverence. While we sat by the ovoo eating a couple more of our remaining biscuits, two large Toyota land cruisers pulled up, full of well-dressed Mongolians, who could only have come from Ulaanbaatar as they conformed to western-style fashion. They parked at the top of the pass and approached the ovoo, facing it in a group. One of them led a prayer before they began worshipping the shrine, with their arms spread out as they made a low-pitched throaty noise. They took it in turned to sprinkle milk on the ovoo before returning to their vehicles.

Two of the group came over to us and offered us some pieces of curd which I was very grateful for, although Phil was less so, since his taste buds still didn t agree with the fermented milk taste. They could speak some English and told us that they were a religious group that were on a pilgrimage to a nearby sacred mountain. They believed that they needed to worship each ovoo on the way to pay their respect to the mountain gods. They believed in a peaceful existence and seemed to be very pleasant people who very quickly gained our deep respect due to their friendly and open nature. They were equally interested in our journey and couldn't believe that we had cycled here from the far west. We parted ways as they continued in the direction we had come, and us in the direction that they had. They had told us that we would ride down a long descent, followed by a short climb, then another descent to the town of Erdenebulgan. Endless wildflower meadows spread out in all directions from the wide dirt track that we rode along. It was a comfortable ride that afternoon and we made fast, if uneventful progress. About ten kilometres out of town, Phil was stung on the inside of his upper leg by a bee, just missing a more critical area! He jumped around in pain and reported that every bump in the road exacerbated it, since his saddle was jarred against the painful area.

We entered the town hoping that we could get hold of some cash at last. Mercifully, the single bank had a cash machine which accepted our debit cards. We were the grateful owners of 300,000 tugrik (about 120 dollars) that would keep us going for most of the next week. Unfortunately, the town's cafés were all shut but there was a large shop in which we bought a lot of food. Now that we could afford to eat as much as we wanted, we both realised how hungry we had been. Two Snickers, one ice cream, a bottle of coke and lots of chocolate biscuits later, we were ready to continue with a new spring in our step. Leaving the town, the road was much wider and seemed to be a major route linking the town with the main road to the south. It climbed alongside another much larger river, which we crossed on a modern bridge. A few kilometres later we were ready to camp. There was no ideal campsite that night, so we found a spot in a muggy overgrown forest that was unfortunately home to a swarm of mosquitoes.

We set up camp on a flat bit of land close to the beautiful river that carved its way through the thick vegetation. We fought our way through the undergrowth to the river bank where we had a wash in the water. It was a wonderful sight. The river ran quickly around a meander, with a low mist rising from its surface. Dew formed on giant spider webs that spanned the distance from one bank to the other. Thick reeds grew on the opposite bank and in the distance, through the thick undergrowth, we could see the gigantic pine forest stretching up the mountainside. Back at the tents we created a stone circle to contain a fire, which we soon had burning. We cooked dinner and were happy to see that the mosquitoes didn't like the smoke. The riding had been fantastic that day, my bike was still working somehow, and the pasta and tea that night was delicious. Life was good.

Animal skin drying in the sun

Morning mist on the hillside

One of many minor river crossings

Perfect singletrack

At the top of the pass in front of the Ovoo

Evening mist on the river

Day 18: Wet, wet, wet
Distance travelled: 78.45 km

The nicest thing about the rain is that it always stops. Eventually.
- Eeyore

I awoke in the wood and for the first time it was raining very heavily at the start of the day. It is very difficult to persuade yourself to get going in such conditions, but we managed to get up, pack the soaking wet tents into our bags and start to ride, without having eaten breakfast. Back on the road we continued up the river valley, dodging puddles and getting soaked. We found a cow shelter after a few miles, so stopped there for breakfast to shelter from the rain. The downpour continued all morning so the whole landscape was completely waterlogged, and the dirt track very difficult to cycle on. It was a good job that we were riding fatbikes which could grip on the muddy loose surface, although we often lost traction. The bottom bracket bodge was still working well despite being wet and covered in dirt.

The track led us away from the thick forest and up a grassy hillside, passing many log cabins that looked warm and inviting. There were lots of dogs that aggressively chased us until we dismounted and squared up to them. The road was unusable for motor vehicles since the surface was too soft and slippery. We were able to continue on our incredible bikes though, albeit slowly. We met only two people that morning; two boys who approached us on horseback warily waving at us, before returning wide grins as we smiled and waved at them. It was an uneventful morning as we climbed around thirty kilometres up the grassy valley passing large herds of animals until finally the rain eased to a very light drizzle and we stopped for lunch.

An undulating landscape of grass-covered hillsides passed by that afternoon, which was quite repetitive although very pretty. Large herds of animals covered the hillsides but most people seemed to be sheltering from the rain. We were using our phones a lot to ensure we were on the right track, since there were so many heading in all directions across the hillsides. My "waterproof" phone turned out not to be and gave up at around two o'clock. The screen turned off for the last time, but annoyingly, the vibrate function still worked and turned itself on. There was nothing I could do to stop it so I stuffed it into my frame bag, trying to muffle the noise. We were now reliant on Phil's phone along with two very large-scale paper maps.

Fortunately, navigation was straightforward after that, as we followed the track up and down a series of hills, until finally we reached the town of Tarialan close to the main road that links Mörön to the cities of Bulgan and Erdenet. On the way in to town we were passed by a dark green coloured motorbike with a sidecar. I couldn't imagine using a sidecar on Mongolian roads; what an uncomfortable experience! The main road was not far away though, perhaps they didn't use it much on the bumpier rural roads. On the way into the town we crossed a river in which we had a quick wash to make ourselves look slightly more presentable, as prior to this we had been covered in mud. We cycled around the town for a few minutes passing a large stadium in the centre, before finding a large relatively modern-looking restaurant. We ordered a three-course feast consisting of a giant potato salad, noodle soup and more buuz.

Five kilometres or so outside of Tarialan we found a good place to camp in the middle of a high grassland. We had the company of lots of grasshoppers that night, which kept hopping into our tents and our food. It was a lovely evening and the sun had finally come out, meaning that I could dry my damp sleeping bag before bed. It was a relatively early time to finish as there were still a couple of hours until sunset, but we didn't want to get any closer to the main road, both hoping for some privacy that night. Our evening had a celebratory feel to it since we had successfully completed our adventurous detour through the remote northern hills. My bottom bracket was still holding out and it was now less critical that it survived as it would be easy for us to get help on the main road. I spent half an hour or so cleaning it out again and reassembling it until it was "*as good as new*"! My phone on the other hand was not! It was still buzzing away but was otherwise completely unresponsive. As we caught up on our diaries and pored over our maps, a large number of cranes passed overhead, gliding across the sky in formation and at high speed. I wondered where they were heading. Just before bed that evening we had a treat in the form of delicious fresh bread from Tarialan, coated in butter and marmalade.

Camping close to Tarailan

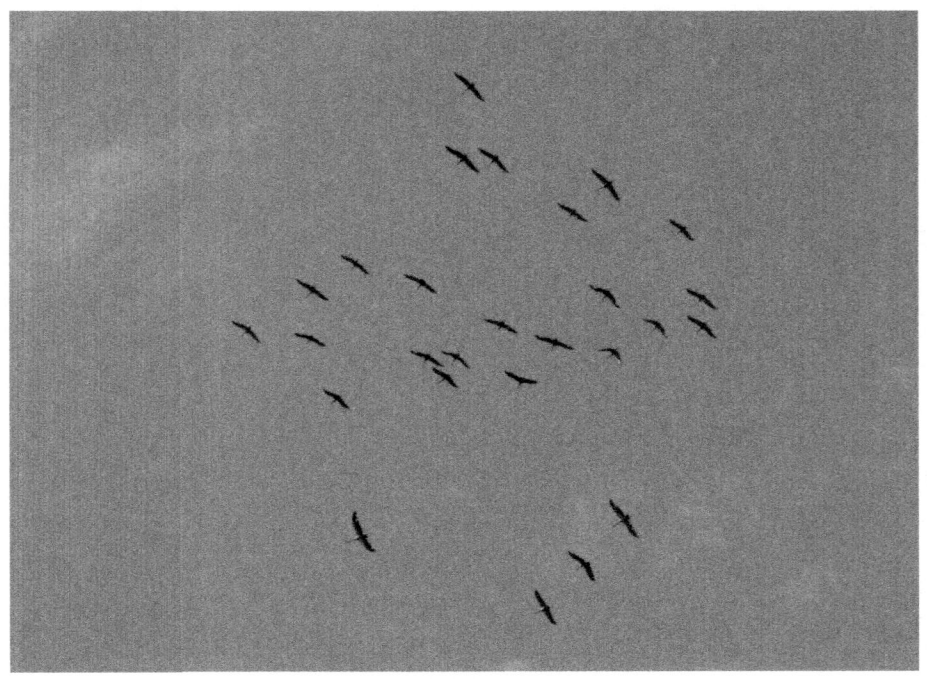

Cranes overhead

Day 19: The longest day
Distance travelled: 115.82 km

Ride as much or as little, or as long or as short as you feel. But ride.
- Eddy Merckx

The day started off very relaxed with a couple of pans of green tea cooked on the resurrected stove. After two kilometres of off-road riding we reached the main road, which was a perfectly smooth two-lane highway. A westerly tailwind boosted our progress as we travelled at around 20 kilometres per hour with ease. Ten kilometres later, my bottom bracket started to seize up again, so I took it apart and spent about 30 minutes trying to insert ball bearings and grease until it spun relatively freely once more. We also both topped our tyres up with air so that they were running at about 20 psi, rather than the usual eight to ten, which upped our average speed considerably since the friction between the tyres and the road was vastly reduced. I had to adjust the bottom bracket a few times that day to encourage it to loosen up, but each time it continued working and the number of kilometres separating us with the Russian border, which would mark the end of our trip, was becoming less and less. Would it hold out?

Climbing slowly in the sunshine we reached a point at which a thick mist hung over the road. As we entered it the temperature dropped considerably, as did the visibility. After putting our coats on we continued, discussing what may have caused the localised mist to sit on the road in this location. Perhaps it had formed because we were reaching the top of a pass, where hotter air from one valley reached the cooler air from the other, causing the water vapour in the air to condense. Making excellent progress, we crossed the pass. This was followed by a long straight descent to the giant Selenge River on its way to Lake Baikal in Russia; the direction in which we were heading.

The ever-present eagles and other hawks were joined by much larger vultures circling overhead. Their relative size was incredible since the vultures dwarfed the eagles that were large themselves. The vultures seemed to be lazy in comparison though and didn't seem to flap their wings very often. The agile hawks could change direction, swooping and diving quickly, whereas the vultures were giant gliders, riding hot air currents to rise and circling down to fall. They are scavengers, so probably live by the road to eat the many offerings of road kill that we saw all too regularly.

Continuing downhill into a low-lying hot wide and beautiful river valley, lined by forested mountains, we reached the small town of Khutag-Undur, which appeared to have developed a local economy as the Mongolian equivalent of a service station. There were a few car garages, shops selling mechanical parts, four or five petrol stations and, most importantly, lots of modern-looking restaurants with much longer menus than we were used to. We enjoyed a beef and potato stew, agreeing that it was excellent not to have to eat mutton for once! Sitting on the table next to us was a family of South Koreans who asked us about our trip, but seemed to have little control over their son who wandered around the restaurant, picking up people's possessions and causing mayhem. Afterwards, Phil visited a shop to purchase food for the afternoon and for dinner, while I rebuilt my bottom bracket for what felt like the hundredth time. This time, I abandoned trying to make the bearing work, simply allowing the crank axle to spin inside the bearing inner cylinder and packing out the gaps between the bearing and the cup with gaffa tape. It really can fix anything!

Continuing along the main road, we crossed a large bridge that overlooked the Selenge river. It was truly spectacular. Looking west from the bridge, there was no sign of civilisation other than a small green-roofed farming hut on the bend of the peaceful, wide river stretching out beneath a deep blue sky. On the other side of the river was a large plain on which a horse race was taking place. We wondered whether this was a local Nadaam festival or just a horse racing event. It was certainly a significant race judging by the substantial number of competitors. As is the norm for Mongolian horse racing, the competitors were all young children who have an advantage due to their low weight. In Mongolia, the jockey is the minor half of the horse/rider pair and the glory of winning a race goes to the horse, not its rider. The endurance of the horses was extremely impressive as we watched the children gallop at full pelt up and down the long grassy course, being filmed by cameramen in jeeps driving alongside.

We bypassed the tollbooth that charged vehicles to cross the river and fortunately it seemed that bikes were exempt. Our road now departed the Selenge and headed south, up another valley following a smaller tributary upstream. The valley was gorgeous, the steep green sides covered with thousands more grazing animals. To begin with the road climbed steeply but then the landscape levelled out and the river meandered across a wide plain with small copses of pine trees forming islands in the great sea of grass. Riding on tarmac was relaxing as there were no bumps to navigate around, and although this would have been boring for a significant length of time, it was a welcome relief for a day or two. Despite what people assume about fatbikes, they are perfectly good at riding on tarmac if the tyres are inflated to high enough pressures. They are perhaps the perfect touring bike, certainly for a wild country like Mongolia.

Approaching the top of the pass, we saw a couple erecting a ger. They had almost built the frame and were in the process of attaching the roof struts. They had picked a ovely spot to settle on a flat grassy meadow, next to a pine forest and near to the river. We crossed another small *service station* town, where we ate a large portion of noodles as we watched vehicles pass on the road. Giant piles of sheepskin were being transported on overloaded lorries and more gers were being transported in the back of pick-up trucks. Lots of motorbikes passed by and the ever-present flow of Toyota Prius' continued, now much more at home on the tarmac road surface.

After buying a couple of bottles of beer at the shop in the town we continued in search for a campsite. My GPS bike computer ticked over 100 kilometres for the day. This was the first time that we had hit three-figures on the trip and was a cause for celebration that evening. The road had left the river behind and it was not for another 15 kilometres that we found a small stream that would provide us with the water we needed for tea and a wash that night. The campsite we settled on was lovely, although in view of the road. There was a verge that obscured us partially but we didn't mind too much. The Mongolians were extremely friendly and we had no reason to hide away that evening. After washing, cooking tea and settling down for supper, we were joined by a group of locals who had pulled off the main road in their Land Cruiser. They approached the river, waved at us and looked unsurprised by our presence. They picked up a few large stones before leaving again. I wondered if they had collected them to add to Ovoos. The other common use for large stones in Mongolia is for cooking marmots. The stones are heated in a fire before the marmot is stuffed with them and the flames are used to burn away the fur. However we had no desire to seek out any more marmot due to the plague risk. After another round of tea and biscuits followed by a delicious beer that had been cooled in the stream, we went to bed. Another great day.

The mighty Selenge

A long distance horse race

Erecting a ger

The main road; Mongolia is developing quickly

Day 20: Bulgan

Distance travelled: 82.93 km

While horse is strong travel to see places
- Mongolian proverb

Phil had a problem that morning when he needed to go to the loo. Our campsite was in full view of the road so he had to wait a while for a gap in the stream of cars that passed. He found a spot and went but unfortunately at that point, a shepherd came over on his horse to investigate our campsite. It was most amusing! We were excited to get going as we would reach the city of Bulgan that day and planned to have a proper break in the afternoon. The sun was shining during breakfast as we packed up our tents and cycled off.

The beautiful main road continued, crossing a high flat plain, on which many families were living in gers near to forest-cladded hills. We met a Spanish couple on touring bikes heading in the direction that we had come from. They had cycled on the road from Erdenet just a couple of days ago, so had not been riding long. They planned to cycle on the main road all the way to Mörön, then head south towards the Gobi Desert, which stretches over most of the south of Mongolia.

The number of birds-of-prey we saw that morning was quite incredible. One roadside sign had seven perched on it, although two took off by the time I managed to get a good photograph. We also saw many more vultures. Watching them take off was very funny. Their vast size means that they find it difficult to get airborne and so need to run along while flapping their wings a bit like an aeroplane getting up to speed on a runway. Eventually when they did struggle off the ground and got up to speed, their slightly panicky, unwieldy take-off routine turned into a graceful glide, which appeared effortless as they quickly gained altitude.

We stopped a few times that morning for buuz and milky tsai, and were enjoying the relaxed feel to the day. The area was becoming more populated, and with the people came large numbers of horses on the roadside, all of which I presumed were owned rather than being wild. Our road passed close to a spectacular extinct volcano, which we could only observe as a perfectly-proportioned hill. There were lots of pictures of the volcano from the air on road signs. With its perfectly circular crater and completely symmetrical conical base it had an 'other-worldly' look to it.

After crossing the plain, a long straight road led us into Bulgan, passing its airport and entering the odd-looking city. We checked into a formerly grand, but now rather tatty-looking hotel. The inside had a hunting-lodge feel to it, with dark wood lined walls and reindeer and stag antlers on the walls. It was very cheap, so we booked a suite for the night, which consisted of three rather impressive rooms, complete with a dining table, large sofa and television (which wasn't working), two large beds and an old, not particularly clean, bathroom. The decor felt a few decades out of date, with tiger-print on the sofas and garish flowery wallpaper. This slightly dated feel of former grandeur was typical of the whole city. The high street was lined with pretty trees planted at equal distances on opposite sides of the road, but their roots had destroyed the pavement all around them, leaving muddy puddles. There were a lot of modern concrete buildings that were looking derelict with many abandoned. Large multi-story hotels looked mostly unoccupied and the whole town, although lived-in and bustling on the main street, felt half empty.

Although Mongolia was never officially part of the Soviet Union, it was very closely aligned to its politics and its fate between 1924-1992, when the country existed as the Mongolian People's Republic. It was, in reality, considered the unofficial 16th republic and operated as a Soviet satellite-state. The Soviet Union controlled most of its internal affairs via a 'puppet leader', who had been appointed by Stalin, named Horloogiyn Chaoybalsan. Following the Soviet Union's example, he introduced a series of *five-year industrial plans*, despite Mongolia's agricultural roots. Mongolian herders were paid to keep a certain number of animals, which were sold for them by the authorities as required. Their salaries were paid, provided they produced an agreed quota of meat and milk. Mongolia was of great strategic importance because it acted as a buffer state between the Soviet Union and China. Fortunately, the vast majority of Mongolia remained untouched by Soviet policies due to its vast size, its inaccessibility and the limited use of its land. Urban areas changed unrecognisably though, and the major city centres now resemble Russian towns with high tower blocks, large concrete monstrosities and wide-open streets.

In the centre of Bulgan we visited a hardware store, which has to be one of the best shops that I have ever been to. A large L-shaped glass top counter contained all manner of enticing items, including fishing equipment, bike bits, knives, car and motorbike parts tools and plumbing components. The shelves lining the walls were a complete mess but the owner seemed to know where everything was. I bought a packet of vacuum-packed grease and some spherical ball bearings to try to improve my bottom bracket. Afterwards we visited an internet café, where I managed to back up my photographs. We then found a restaurant and ordered a gigantic meal, with starters and two main courses, each of which was meant for two. We had beef and pork cooked in a Chinese style; stir-fried and spicy. Upstairs the restaurant had its own karaoke bar, which seems to be a national pastime in the cities. Around twenty people came and went, to use their own karaoke booth. This seemed to us, an odd early afternoon's activity. The sounds coming from upstairs confirmed that Mongolian karaoke is of no better quality than ours. A couple of beers later, we were ready to head back to the hotel. On the way back we saw a gigantic off-road motorhome with a German number plate. It must have been worth a fortune, with giant knobbly tyres, a satellite dish on the roof and what looked like armour plating! I couldn't help but think that the travel experience would have been somewhat diminished in such a vehicle. Back at the hotel I fixed my bottom bracket once again, this time I repacked the bearing with the steel balls that I had bought and it span again. I was now feeling quite confident that it would survive.

The hotel had a billiards room with an excellent full-size snooker table which we used for an hour or so. There was also a large nightclub downstairs which, as we went to bed, was filling up with well-dressed young locals. One more beer and a large piece of cake later, we were ready for a good night's sleep in a comfortable bed. Bulgan had been a great place to visit, although also a reminder of the challenge that Mongolia's traditional lifestyle faces in trying to exist within the modern world. This city certainly felt the furthest place from rural Mongolia that we had visited on our trip so far.

Hawk infestation

Giant vultures

A delicious meal in Bulgan

The billiards room in our hotel in Bulgan

Day 21: Erdenet
Distance travelled: 57.66 km

Greed keeps men forever poor, even the abundance of this world will not make them rich
- Mongolian proverb

Taking a back route out of Bulgan gave us an insight to life in its suburbs. People either lived in pine cabins situated on fenced-off rectangular shaped blocks of land, or in gers. Animals wandered around the neighbourhood, and most people seemed to own a horse despite living in the city. The boundary between city and countryside wasn't obvious because the density of people's homes decreased slowly until we were back in the grasslands. For the first few kilometres of the day, we decided to follow the old main road out of Bulgan to avoid riding on the new tarmac. The track took us out of the east side of Bulgan, across a river that was lined with animals drinking, then up the other side of the valley and out of the city. The old road had deteriorated, becoming a gravel track that climbed steeply over a large pass back to the main road. On top of a hill was a large mast, probably used for mobile phone broadcasting.

After around half an hour of difficult climbing, we reached the pass and quickly descended on a rutted, eroded road. Soon we were back on the main road that links Bulgan to its larger neighbour, Erdenet. The main road was great to cycle on, with a perfect surface low levels of traffic and a large gap between the carriageway and road edge, more than wide enough for us to ride in. A tailwind helped our progress and we were well rested after our evening in Bulgan. Things were looking up! The road passed through undulating countryside, beautifully green and fertile, still used by hundreds of people living the traditional nomadic lifestyle, despite their proximity to the modern life of the inhabitants of the nearby cities. Old vehicle tracks had formed parallel ruts either side of the road, presumably formed by passing traffic before the tarmac was laid.

The Mongolian government is driving a nationwide road-development program, which started in Ulaanbaatar and spread to the surrounding cities. They plan to develop this further and link many of the inaccessible rural areas to the cities with tarmac roads. I have mixed feelings about the development of the country. From the government's and city-dweller's points of view, the country needs to develop quickly to catch up with the rest of world and make use of its significant natural resources in order to boost its economy. From the traditional nomad's point of view, developing the country is an environmental disaster and of no benefit. Nomads are facing a crisis, partly due to their dwindling numbers and partly due to climate change, which is causing harsher and harsher winters.

Every few years Mongolia suffers a particularly harsh winter, known as the zud. It used to occur once every decade, but now is happening more and more frequently. During the zud, Mongolians lose millions of their livestock, which is their only source of food, transportation and income. As a result, each time a zud hits, nomads are forced to give up their way of life and move to the cities. Overselling of livestock before winter arrives has now caused the cost of meat to fall by 50 percent and the nomads' existence is under threat. State support for the nomads is vital during these winters and it would be great if the country could become an example of sustainable development to the world, developing in a way that doesn't change the traditional lifestyle and maintains its wonderful environment and culture. Mongolia is a victim of the global habits which lead to climate change, being a very low emitter of carbon dioxide itself, with the exception of Ulaanbaatar where winter smogs are commonplace.

Back on the road, we reached the top of another small climb where a friendly lady and her daughter were selling blueberries on the roadside. We stopped and bought a couple of bags, asking where they picked them by miming. They pointed up to a woodland on the top of the nearby hill. The blueberries were presented in large jars sitting on a homemade wooden bench. The ladies sat on Coleman fold-out camping chairs, or perhaps a cheap replica from a local market. It seemed that they had quite a successful business since their money tin was quite full, but they looked very bored, sitting on the roadside all day. We passed them two pieces of cake from Bulgan as we waved goodbye, for which they seemed very grateful.

The two cities are separated by only 60 kilometres, which seems a tiny distance in such a large country. It didn't take us long to cycle between them on the tarmac road, so we arrived on the outskirts of Erdenet at around lunchtime. Erdenet was an impressive sight as we approached and had the feel of a giant metropolis compared to what we had become accustomed to during the previous weeks. Around 83,000 people live in the city, which makes it the third largest in the country after Ulaanbaatar (over one million), and Darkhan (around 150,000). It took around 20 minutes to pass through the sprawling suburbs of colourfully-roofed wooden bungalows sitting in fenced, or sometimes walled, rectangular compounds. Large billboards advertised restaurants and hotels and the whole place had an upbeat feel to it, appearing much more economically successful than nearby Bulgan.

Erdenet is a young city, founded in 1974, due to the discovery of large copper deposits and the subsequent development of one of the world's largest copper mines. The name "Erdenet" means *treasure* after the underground source of wealth that had been discovered. Many engineers and miners moved to the city, over 50 percent of whom were Russian. When the Soviet Union fell most Russians returned to their home country, although there are still around 8,000 Russians in Erdenet. The city is linked to the trans-Mongolian Railway, which itself is linked to Russia. The giant mine is incredibly important to the country's economy, responsible for around 14 percent of its GDP and employing 8,000 people. It is also a source of controversy, since many traditional Mongolians consider it sacrilegious to spoil the natural beauty of their country. The Russian government owned 49% of the mine for 25 years after the fall of the Soviet Union, until in 2016, Vladimir Putin issued an executive order to transfer the stake to a private, state-owned company. It is generally considered that Mongolia has not benefitted proportionally to the scale of the mine.

Reaching the centre, it was clear that the city had been heavily influenced by the Soviet Union, judging by the large concrete tower blocks lining wide multi-lane roads, and imposing grand, ugly, but functional buildings. Checking into a cheap hotel, we showered, got changed then went to explore the city on foot. The main street felt a million miles away from the Mongolian steppe, with modern cars, immaculately-kept roadside paths, fashionably dressed inhabitants, cosmopolitan restaurants and shops and large malls. We entered a supermarket, which had a large variety of products available, comparable to a large grocery shop in Europe. A restaurant served a great variety of food, and there were lots of bars, even a cute little bakery, where we bought a cupcake each. We passed a giant sports centre with the Olympic rings on a scaffold frame on its roof. A large cycling club passed, with young people dressed in lycra, riding good quality road bikes. Inside the mall there were lots of stalls selling cheap tacky bags, clothes and many other products. Higher quality shops selling genuine goods were common too, but the products were more expensive than they would have been in Europe.

After a couple of hours exploring the pleasant, but highly contrasting lifestyle of the people in the city of Erdenet, we returned to our hotel and relaxed for a couple of hours before dinner. Planning the next section of the trip, we decided we had enough time left to make a detour to Mongolia's most famous Buddhist monastery, which would involve turning off the main road the next day and heading north into the countryside once more. Dinner was fantastic; we each had a large burger with cheese melted over it, along with French fries and a tasty fresh salad. City life has its benefits! The Mongolian dubbed version of Lord of the Rings on the television was slightly annoying though, so after a single beer, we left the restaurant. The hotel bar was filling up because this hotel also had its own nightclub on the floor below. We headed up to bed. I struggled to get to sleep with the ever-present background noise of karaoke coming from various locations in the city.

Blueberries on the roadside

Entering Erdenet

Day 22: Off-road again

Distance travelled: 110.00 km

From the air Mongolia looks like God's preliminary sketch for earth, not so much a country as the ingredients out of which countries are made: grass, rock, water and wind.

- Stanley Stewart, In the Empire of Genghis Khan

Although looking forward to resuming our adventurous exploration of the remote Mongolian countryside, we weren't quite ready to leave the comforts of the city when we checked out of our hotel. As we cycled out of Erdenet, we visited a modern café for breakfast where we ordered toasted paninis, pancakes and delicious freshly ground coffee. Leaving the city on its east side involved cycling through a giant area of industrial development. Large pipes lined the roadside, covered in several inches of insulation. They were coming from a coal fired power plant that was built by the Soviet Union in 1986. It is a combined heat and power plant that now generates 50 megawatts of electricity, having recently been extended from the original size of 20 megawatts. The hot water left over after the steam that turns the electric turbines has condensed, is used to heat buildings in the city, rather than being wasted in cooling towers.

We passed the giant complex of the Erdenet Copper Mine to the south of the road, and then a large railway station. A massive dam and reservoir were built to the north of the road, which was lined with garages and other small businesses. Finally we left the industry behind and the city faded back into the beautiful Mongolian countryside. On the way out of the city, we met two Spanish touring cyclists, who had just arrived on a train from Ulaanbaatar They were planning to cycle to Khövsgöl Nuur, possibly taking the same route that we had, so were very interested to hear about where we had been. When cycle touring, one of the best ways to find out about the road ahead is by talking about it with other cyclists, whom you almost always meet at some point.

Leaving the city behind in glorious sunshine, the road led down to a small river, then over a couple of small passes to another much larger river along a wide flat floodplain. At the top of each pass was a Buddhist shrine marking the point at which the road began its descent back to the wildflower filled grasslands that stretched as far as the eye could see. By late morning the temperature had increased and the air was humid and uncomfortably muggy, but then the sky became slightly overcast, lowering the temperature slightly and making the riding more comfortable. We covered 60 kilometres that morning, after which we stopped for lunch at a little café inside a ger that sold excellent buuz. Each kilometre that we covered was marked by a little blue sign on the roadside, counting up from the zero marker at Erdenet. We stopped at a shop to restock on supplies for the off-road section that laid ahead then continued until 81 kilometres after Erdenet, where we reached a turning to the north. We left the main road to follow a smaller track that would lead us to Ambayasgalent Khiid, the large monastery we planned to reach the following day.

There were lots of mosquitoes at the point at which we turned off the main road. We had not been expecting such a major junction and it seemed that a lot of traffic travelled to the monastery. A new tarmac road was under construction but wasn't yet ready for traffic, so we cycled on a good dirt track across the steppe. The riding was very unpleasant in the muggy, mosquito infested air, as we climbed and descended five passes back-to-back. The wide-open grasslands were beautiful but soon gave way to large wheat fields, which were an incredible contrast to what we had passed through during the previous couple of weeks. This was the first example of wide-scale farming in this Northern region of Mongolia.

Climbing the last pass, we overtook a vehicle that was struggling to make headway up the steep road and smelling strongly of burning clutch. Another vehicle had a flat tyre. Our fatbikes continued through the difficult terrain with no problems, including my bottom bracket that was still holding out very well. At the top of the last pass we were treated to our first view over the stunningly beautiful grass covered plain surrounding Ambayasgalent Khiid. A meandering river crossed the centre of the plain, on which thousands of animals grazed, dozens of gers were erected and hundreds of people were living. It was an idyllic situation and obvious why so many people had decided to settle there.

We descended on the road, then continued off-road for a couple of kilometres until we found a lovely flat spot of grass next to the river. After pitching our tent we heated a pan of instant coffee, which we shared with a nomad who had come over to investigate. There was no word of thanks; not because he was ungrateful, but because sharing is expected. When he came over to sit with us, he had become our guest. We spent a while that evening planning our route the following day. If all went to plan we would arrive at the monastery early in the morning, have a look round and then head north on a track that we knew existed as it was on Google Earth, but was not marked on any of our maps. The next day would be a real adventure! Pasta was most welcome that evening followed by three rounds of tea made from boiled river water. Another fantastic day.

The Soviet built Erdenet Thermal Power Plant

More Buuz

Another lovely riverside campsite

Our evening visitor

Day 23: Trailblazing
Distance travelled: 91.91 km

The distance between heaven and earth is no greater than one thought
- Mongolian proverb

The day began with bread and Nutella in the centre of the plain filled with animals, gers and nomads on horseback... not a bad start. Cycling along a lovely grassy track that ran between twenty or so gers built on either side, we waved good morning to lots of nomad families on the seven-kilometre ride to the Buddhist Monastery, Ambayasgalent Khiid. When we arrived at the front gates at around nine o'clock the monastery was not yet open. A tour guide who was hanging around the front entrance told us that it would not open until ten o'clock. A small collection of buildings and gers were built to the west of the monastery so we went to explore. It seemed that most inhabitants were not up yet, so most of the shops were shut. Getting up late seemed to be fairly typical for Mongolians everywhere in the country. One small shop was open though, so we went inside to see what we could get to eat. Amazingly the young lady working there could speak English, which is very unusual for remote Mongolia. She prepared two large pot noodles for us, along with instant coffee, while telling us about her life. She was working in her mother's shop in her home village, as she did each summer. For most of the year she studied at Beijing University, but she always came back for the summer holiday on the Trans-Mongolian railway that crosses the Gobi Desert. It must be an epic train journey.

After eating our second breakfast, we cycled back over to the monastery, which had now been opened. It is a large and beautiful building that is home to monks from the school of Tibetan Buddhism. Its name means "*the monastery of tranquil felicity*" and it is considered to be one of the three most important Buddhist institutions in the country, as well as the most attractive and architecturally interesting. The complex was built in 1737, and is well preserved despite a general feeling of decay. Unfortunately, the monks are unable to keep it maintained due to their dwindling numbers. UNESCO have renovated the buildings and are contributing to their maintenance, but like most religious institutions in the country it was tragically affected by Soviet purges. In 1937 many of the outer buildings were destroyed and most of the monks were executed. In 1936 two thousand monks lived at the monastery, but now there are just 30. During the purges many of the valuable artefacts and manuscripts were looted. Fortunately, however, the main building remained untouched, possibly due to a sympathetic local commander., As a result many of the hidden artefacts were not found. We explored the various temples, admired the artwork and watched the monks meditating in the large central chamber. It was a remarkably peaceful place but felt empty, given its large size and few inhabitants. Despite this, we could appreciate the beautifully decorated buildings with their carved wooden beams, ornately painted columns and gold covered dragons on each roof corner. The whole complex is symmetrical and surrounded by high walls. It was an extremely interesting and thought-provoking place.

After leaving the monastery we returned to the small adjacent village to attempt to find out more information about our onward route, and to restock on supplies. Looking around the buildings, we came across a family of four generations sitting around a stove, on which a large steel bowl full of boiling oil sat simmering away. A production line was in place for the manufacture of deep-fried dough. The finished product was made from two long strips twisted around each other to make a plaited pattern. Two young children helped their mother knead the dough and roll it into strips. Their grandmother appeared to oversee twisting the strips around one another, before passing them on to her father, who sat by the pan and deep-fried batch after batch. He waved us over and offered us a couple to taste. They were very nice, being similar to doughnuts but without the sugar coating. We asked about the road to the north of the monastery that wasn't marked on our map by saying the name of a town, which we knew was situated to the north. They nodded, but looked at our bikes worried. The mother of the young children thought we would be able to make it, but nobody else seemed to agree. That was good enough for us, we would give it a try!

After a quick trip to a poorly-stocked shop, in which we bought a few calorific snacks and some dried noodles, we returned to the family and asked to buy a bag of their twisted doughnuts to take with us. The old man put about thirty of them into a plastic bag and passed them to us, but looked shocked when I tried to offer him money for them. He wouldn't take any and with a giant smile on his face waved farewell to us. What a wonderful family! Heading north and feeling good about the world, we started to climb over a ridge-line at the top of a range of hills. Looking back over the gorgeous plain with the beautiful monastery in the foreground, was another unforgettable view in this staggeringly beautiful country. We followed a minor track up to the top of the ridge where it disappeared, giving way to the endless sea of grass. Continuing downhill we headed for the bottom of the valley, which we planned to follow as it seemed to be pointing in the right direction.

Near the bottom of the valley we bumped into two horsemen. It appeared they had never seen such a bizarre sight, as they stared at us in disbelief. Smiling and waving appeared to remove them from their trance, after which they enthusiastically greeted us and did all they could to encourage us that we were heading in the right direction; good news because we didn't really know where the valley was leading. As we left they shouted *Daagent* to us, which was encouraging as that was the name of the village we were heading towards. After a couple of kilometres of cycling along the grassy floor of the valley, we entered a forest at which point a proper track began, which was easier to follow and had a much better riding surface.

The forest trail turned out to be a fantastic cross-country mountain biking route, as it climbed a pass, wound through trees and along a river valley, then down a steep descent with natural banked corners and rocky features to keep things interesting. The trees thinned out as the track led onto grassy pastures, on which around a dozen gers were built. The dogs in that area were particularly fierce and we had a couple of show-down exchanges with the bravest. Cycling past the gers, we first heard a bark, then scampering footsteps followed by growling and more barking. At this point what we really wanted to do was pedal quickly and try to outrun the dogs, but they were quick. We squared up to them, threw stones and eventually (usually) they would run away. In one case, though, this didn't work and we had a standoff with the dog for a couple of minutes, until the owner came over and rescued us!

We passed through the ger-filled pastures and crossed a sodden plain. The wet ground was a breeding ground for mosquitoes, so the next couple of hours were thoroughly uncomfortable. No amount of deet could keep the flying devils at bay. Crossing the muddy marshy grassland, it was almost a relief to reach a solid track that climbed steeply up a pass. It turned out to be worse though, since the hot muggy weather combined with the added exertion led to a large amount of salty sweat dripping into my eyes, and the slower speed led to even more mosquito bites. All in all, it was a thoroughly unpleasant experience, although looking back on it is oddly satisfying! After crossing three small passes, a very long climb up and over a fourth followed. Passing a bewildered looking man on a motorbike and having cycled for over half an hour up a very steep, little used dirt track, we topped out on the final pass and began a descent to a much more pleasant, and typically Mongolian green valley. The comforting sight of gers and grazing animals greeted us once more.

Skirting the edge of a hillside, we decided to stop trailblazing and head east to a more well used track. The main reason for this is that if we carried on north we had no way of knowing if there was a way of crossing either the Selenge or the Orkhon rivers. The Selenge was currently to our east, and the Orkhon to our west. To the north was their confluence and there was no way of fording either, since they are both very large. After the confluence the then much larger Selenge continues its journey north into Russia, where it widens until it reaches its delta on the edge of Lake Baikal. According to our map and the satellite images we had found on Google Earth, there was a small car ferry that took vehicles across the Orkhon to the west, so that was where we were heading.

The road was wider and better used, leading through giant fields of wheat full of buzzing insects. Recent rain had turned the dirt track into a slippery muddy mess, which we struggled to progress on; sliding all over the place. Judging by the tyre marks, lots of cars had skidded and spun around on the road too. After twenty-or-so non-eventful kilometres of undulating road, we eventually arrived in the town of Khushaat, on the edge of the Orkhon River. Straight away we headed to a café, where we were welcomed by a motherly owner who didn't ask what we wanted, but started cooking a meal for us before showing us to a table. Twenty minutes later we were tucking into a giant mountain of rice, mutton stew, potato salad and two beers. The perfect end to a tough, but rewarding day!

While we were eating, the door to a back room opened and three very drunk ladies came out and met a man who was drinking at the bar. They had a bottle of vodka with them, which was virtually empty. The man went over to a giant sound system with metre high speakers and started playing very loud and appalling Western dance music possibly for our *benefit*. The ladies began dancing and drinking even more! Soon after this we decided to leave, heading out of town along the western bank of the Orkhon. Looking for a place to camp, we cycled quickly downhill to the river, but when we stopped we were instantly set upon by swarms of mosquitoes that clearly bred close to the water. Quickly turning around, we retraced our bike tracks a couple of kilometres to the main road, then headed up the slope at the bottom of a mountain, away from the river. We pitched our tents and immediately went inside to escape the flying torturous insects that were still present, although in lower numbers on this higher land. It had been an incredible day, with highs and lows, and some of the best mountain biking that we had experienced in Mongolia.

The main temple

Ambayasgalent Khiid

Making the donut-like snacks

Leaving the monastery behind

A mosquito-infested climb

Muddy tracks through the steppe

Day 24: Total washout
Distance travelled: 89.34 km

There is no good in anything until it is finished
- Genghis Khan

It rained all night, but fortunately my tent stayed dry inside. Phil was less comfortable, with a large puddle around his feet that morning. We breakfasted in his larger tent again, to shelter from mosquitoes and drizzle. There was a brief respite from the rain for an hour or so, giving us a window to pack up and set off, but after an hour or so, it started again with a vengeance.

We were approaching the point at which we hoped the large wooden raft that took cars across the Orkhon was located. Looking forward to seeing how it worked, we were disappointed to find that a large new bridge had been built. The area north of Ulaanbaatar, linking the country to Russia, is now developing very quickly with expanding towns, tarmac roads, a well-used railway and growing infrastructure. Infrastructure development is changing this part of the country significantly, and many of the people living here will never return to the nomadic existence of their recent ancestors.

After around 15 kilometres of riding along wet sandy tracks, we reached the main tarmac road, which was a wide two-lane carriageway. At the junction a Mongolian herder came over to us on a battered old motorbike, with his large herd of sheep and goats. He spent about five minutes staring at us. We waved but he didn't respond, looking as though he had seen a ghost. Eventually he nodded h s head at us before moving on with his animals. Phil reattached his panniers, which had become dislodged, before we began riding on the main road. We would not be riding off-road again on this adventure and given the weather, this was no bad thing.

The rain continued over the course of the day and we became completely drenched. The wind was blowing against us as we cycled north towards the Russian border. It was clear that Mongolia was not going to let us leave without putting up a fight! The day was uneventful. We had a very tasty noodle soup in a roadside ger, which we paid far too much for, but we had no choice as we had forgotten to ask the price before eating the food. We climbed and descended a few minor passes stopping to eat honey and bread a few times, and all the time looking at the map to see how we were getting on. Chatting over a honey sandwich, it was clear that we were both of the opinion that we were making very slow progress and rather keen to reach the town of Sukhbaatar, which would mark the end of the cycling on our trip. We weren't having much fun!

The torrential downpour continued, and the wind picked up, now so strong that we were cycling into horizontal rain which stung our faces as it hit. The endless straight road turned west, momentarily giving us some respite from the rain, which was now hitting us from the side. A second corner realigned us so that we were heading north again, battling the onslaught again. It was difficult to cycle down a hill, on which our top speed was just nine kilometres per hour. Eventually we reached the outskirts of the industrial town of Sukhbaatar, which we crawled into between giant grain storage containers, large factories, and a giant railway junction. We entered the first hotel that we could find, booked a room and had a cold shower since the hot water wasn't working – just the thing after a freezing day in torrential rain!

We walked to the nearby train station to find out if it was possible to book a ticket to Ulan-Ude, the city in Russia that we would be flying out from in three days' time. After getting very confused and trying to interpret Cyrillic writing, while attempting not to get into a conversation with the local drunks, we gave up and asked for help from a very helpful English-speaking soldier. He told us that we would need to return early in the morning to buy a ticket and that the next train left at 11 o'clock the following day. Leaving the station, we went to a couple of shops to buy some presents. An immaculate shop with a large showroom sold fine clothes, furniture and kitchens, but didn't have anything suitable. Named the "*style factory*", it was very odd to see such a modern-looking shop in Mongolia, and felt a million miles away from the Buddhist Monastery we had left the previous morning. The next-door supermarket proved to be a much better place to buy presents. We bought bottles of vodka (named Chinghiss of course) as presents, and lots of snacks for our train journey the next day. Olympics on the television along with a beer, followed by a celebratory meal ended our last evening in Mongolia. What a trip!

The trans-Mongolian railway and Ulan-Uud
Distance travelled (by bike) 1.06 km

Up early, we scoffed down a reasonable breakfast in the hotel and cycled through the continuing downpour to Sukhbaatar Railway Station. We managed to purchase tickets by pointing at a clock and repeatedly saying *"Ulan-Ude"*, before sitting in the waiting room not really knowing what to do. We both assumed that the staff would let us know when we should make our way to the train to board it, since it was very quiet, and they had motioned for us to sit down. Eventually, after waiting for about 45 minutes, we decided to find out what was going on outside on the platform. Two carriages were parked up at the platform and there was frantic activity outside. A stressed looking guard came over to us and motioned to us that we needed to rush down to the train, looking at us like we were fools! It seemed that we had left things very late and that we were supposed to be there well before now.

One carriage appeared to be Russian and the other Mongolian. The Mongolian guard looked much more approachable than the formidable Russian lady with red lipstick and a stern face. The kindly looking Mongolian looked very concerned when she saw us however. She shook her head and wagged her finger at our bikes, telling us in no uncertain terms that there was no chance we would be allowed to board as there was clearly no room. The Russian lady just looked down at us from the door of the train as if we were completely stupid to even contemplate entering her carriage. We had no chance at all of boarding there. Showing our ticket to the Mongolian lady seemed to work, I boarded the train and she showed me our cabin. Returning, I gave the good news to Phil and we proceeded to lift the bikes onto the train, thinking we would be allowed to put them in the carriage entrance space. However, when they realised what we were doing, we were almost pushed off the train. We were allowed on but our bikes weren't! I couldn't believe it; did they expect us to leave our bikes behind?

Phil took matters into his own hands, trying a different tactic. He approached a man on the platform, who seemed to be in charge and in army uniform. They had a laugh together and the guy was very interested in our bikes, so Phil offered him a go. He spent about five minutes riding around the platform. I was getting very anxious because the carriages were being attached to an engine at that point. They were clearly getting ready to leave. After a few selfies with the army guards and a chance for a couple more of them to have a go on the fatbikes, the problem was solved! The *boss*, who was a very smiley happy and friendly chap, had a word with the Mongolian train guard, who opened the doors at the other end of the carriage and smiled at us as we lifted out bikes onto the train. We sat in our seats as the train pulled off just a couple of minutes later. Things work differently in Mongolia!

Two guys entered the carriage, both a similar age to us. They were Germans who had just rafted down the Selenge River, which coincidently had been something we had considered doing if my bottom bracket had been irreparable. One of them had just finished an internship working with the Mongolian forestry department on a project to encourage sustainable tree-felling. His friend had come to join him for a holiday with a difference. They had bought plastic barrels, wood and rope from a market, constructed their own raft and spent the last ten days floating down the river. What an adventure; perhaps one for the future! They were good company for the hours we spent on the train to Russia. We shared stories, experiences and food, which helped pass the time.

After leaving Sukhbaatar, the Russian border was only around 15 kilometres away. We then had a long wait while luggage and passports were checked and dogs came on board, presumably checking for drugs. After the extremely friendly Russian customs officers had finished the search, we were allowed to leave the carriage. We were back on Russian soil once more, with about three hours to kill until the train was ready to leave again. It was a welcome treat to visit a Russian café in the tiny town where the train had stopped. The menu had six pages and, compared to the standard fare of mutton stew or dumplings we had been eating for the past month, it was paradise!

Back on the train, the spectacular scenery whizzed past outside. We followed the Selenge, traversed through miles of Siberian steppe, rounded a large lake, then entered the large metropolis of Ulan-Ude. Exiting the train at the bustling station felt strange, having been in one of the most remote countries on earth for so long. There were trains from all over Russia waiting on platforms and hundreds of people in western-style clothes rushing around. We drew lots of looks and smiles as we pushed our fatbikes through the station. Cycling out onto the street, we quickly found a hotel and checked in for the three nights we had left before we would fly home to England.

While in Ulan-Ude we visited many of the sights and sampled excellent food, including delicious fresh fish from Lake Baikal. There were a few interesting museums, the highlight was one full of Buddhist artwork which included some rather strange sculptures, including one of two men having a pee. We looked around a pretty orthodox church and walked around a city park. We ate in a surprisingly cheap revolving restaurant at the top of a 5-star hotel one evening, and at another high-end hotel the next where we drank *vesper martinis*. The most memorable landmark was the gigantic head of Lenin in the main square. This totally bizarre monument is the largest version of his head in existence, made out of bronze and weighing 42 tonnes! The size of the landmarks left behind are directly proportional to the influence of the Soviet ruler. Lenin has certainly been further immortalised by Ulan-Ude's eight-metre-high monstrosity. Bizarrely, Lenin's head is now a popular backdrop for inhabitants of the city to have in their wedding photos!

On the whole, Ulan-Ude was a surprisingly metropolitan busy and varied city. The quality of life seemed high there and the locals were extremely friendly. It was much larger than we had been expecting and was a perfect place to end our trip, providing places to celebrate and to arrange the logistics of getting the bikes back home. We found a large sports shop, who's friendly assistant gave us two cardboard bike boxes in which to pack them. All too soon though, it was time to head back home. Although I feel this way at the end of every biking adventure, this time I can say without a doubt that Mongolia had provided the best cycle touring of any country I have ever been to. It is a wonderful part of the world. My overwhelming memory of the country is the freedom enjoyed by its wonderful friendly inhabitants in its vast open spaces. It is a country that you can travel across for days without seeing a fence, and one which has changed very little in the last few thousand years. I hope that Mongolia remains the greatest wilderness on earth for many years to come.

On board the Trans-Siberian Railway

Just across the Russian border

The largest sculpture of Lenin's head in the world

Celebrating in style

Looking back on the trip, one year on

Greed keeps men forever poor, even the abundance of this world will not make them rich

- Mongolian proverb

It has taken over a year to write this book and as ever things have been unbelievably busy. Real life is great. I live in Sheffield with my wife Laura, ride bikes every week with my mates in the Peak District and work as a physics teacher. My school have recently let me build a mountain bike track on the ground, so I'm trying to spread the biking bug to the next generation. I have been on lots of other short adventures, including bikepacking trips riding up Snowdon and Helvelyn, a six-day bikepacking tour of the Scottish Highlands and a five-week backpacking trip around Peru and Ecuador, including hiking the Inca Trail to Maccu Pichu. Trips like Mongolia and the Indian Himalaya tour I did a couple of years earlier are wonderful experiences, but don't seem real during day-to-day life. They are isolated events, that provide perspective on life and how fortunate we are in the western world.

Weather, politics and work are probably the three main sources of complaint in Britain, but in comparison to Mongolia, we have it extremely good. In our country, it is always safe and comfortable outside; in Mongolia it reaches -40 ºC in winter and can reach +40 ºC in summer. Add to that the fact that most Mongolians have to keep herds of livestock alive, don't have a mains fuel or water supply and have to deal with swarms of mosquitoes in the hot months. Politics-wise, changing governments in Britain do have a small effect on our daily lives, but in Mongolia most people are forgotten by their state. If you're old and ill in the middle of the Steppe in midwinter, your chances aren't great. A Brit is likely to live 12 years longer than a Mongolian. Our NHS is wonderful, our education system is unbelievable, the opportunities we have are incredible. Not so for most people in Mongolia. In terms of work, Mongolian nomads look after hundreds of sheep and goats and move their families around to find grass for them, which may prove to be a waste of time if the *zud* arrives. We have incredible opportunities in comparison.

BUT

Mongolian community values trump ours and that of all other more-economically-developed- countries that I have visited. Partly by necessity and partly due to their warm and friendly nature, Mongolians are wonderful people, whose first thought when they see a stranger is *how can I help them*. They rely on their neighbours and work together to survive. I feel that many people in Britain (and the western world) are losing this due to televisions, the internet and locked doors. This is sad.

The opportunity to visit Mongolia was fantastic and the adventure eye-opening, immensely enjoyable but perhaps most of all, incredibly humbling. To experience the Mongol an nomadic way-of-life first-hand is something that I will never forget. I am very grateful for all the help that the nomads gave us, and thankful to Phil for his excellent company once again.

To see more of my pictures, watch Go-Pro videos of parts of the trip and to read about my other adventures, including my bike ride around the world, please visit www.tombrucecycling.com.

Thanks very much for reading.

Printed in Great Britain
by Amazon